Design in Puritan American Literature

William J. Scheick

Design in Puritan American Literature

THE UNIVERSITY PRESS OF KENTUCKY

Frontispiece: the frontispiece
of *Emblems* (1635) by Frances Quarles.

Copyright © 1992 by The University Press of Kentucky

Scholarly publisher for the Commonwealth,
serving Bellarmine College, Berea College, Centre
College of Kentucky, Eastern Kentucky University,
The Filson Club, Georgetown College, Kentucky
Historical Society, Kentucky State University,
Morehead State University, Murray State University,
Northern Kentucky University, Transylvania University,
University of Kentucky, University of Louisville,
and Western Kentucky University.

Editorial and Sales Offices: Lexington, Kentucky 40508-4008

Library of Congress Cataloging-in-Publication Data

Scheick, William J.
  Design in Puritan American literature / William J. Scheick.
    p. cm.
  Includes bibliographical references and index.
  ISBN 978-0-8131-5424-4
  1. American literature—Puritan authors—History and criticism.
  2. American literature—Colonial period, ca. 1600-1775—History and criticism. 3. American literature—New England—History and criticism. 4. Christian literature, American—History and criticism. 5. Puritans—New England—Intellectual life.
  6. Rhetoric—1500-1800 I. Title.
PS153.P87S34 1992
810.9'001—dc20   91-35585

This book is printed on recycled acid-free

For Catherine
and
for Jessica and Nathan

Contents

Introduction	1
1. The Necessity of Language	6
Words Like Wooden Horses	
William Bradford and Thomas Morton	6
Double-Talk	
Renaissance and Reformed Traditions	19
Concealed Verbal Artistry	
Richard Mather and Edward Taylor	23
2. The Winding Sheet of Meditative Verse	30
The Wrack of Mortal Poets	
Anne Bradstreet's "Contemplations"	35
Unfolding the Twisting Serpent	
Edward Taylor's "Meditation 1.19"	45
3. Laughter and Death	68
All in Jest	
Nathaniel Ward's The Simple Cobler	69
Dissolving Stones	
Urian Oakes's Elegy on Thomas Shepard	80
4. Breaking Verbal Icons	89
Nature, Reason, and Language	
Jonathan Edwards in Reaction	90
From Something to Nothing to Everything	
Edwards's Early Sermons	103
5. Islands of Meaning	120
Eighteenth-Century Allegory or Satire?	
Nathan Fiske's "An Allegorical Description"	121
The Letter Killeth	
Edward Bellamy's "To Whom This May Come"	130
Notes	146
Index	164

Introduction

In this study I focus on several Puritan American writings as texts that invite *reading*, interpretation. I agree with J. Hillis Miller's surprising but welcome recent argument for an academic return to an awareness of the text as a text. Before moving students into abstract realms of literary discourse, Miller contends, critics are obliged first of all to return to the "traditional task" of "the teaching of *reading*," the training of their students "in reading all the signs."[1] Such a reminder is reinforced by Dominick LaCapra's related response to critical approaches to literature that emphasize only its expression of unconscious repression. Equally important, LaCapra observes, is the consideration of the artistic implications of (somewhat recoverable) conscious authorial intention; for every writer expresses some intention in his or her work.[2] Although I engage certain contextual matters in my discussion, as anyone studying Puritan literature must, I am not interested here in furthering the scholarly tendency to read colonial American works "historically" as documents principally providing a direct record of their time or "new historically" as documents primarily representing various kinds of psychological, gender, or political repression in their time. Both of these foci have value; but too often they slight another rich attribute of these works. In some of their writings the Puritans also engaged aesthetic concerns that apparently were for them profoundly important. My study explores one feature of this aesthetic dimension of their work.

In constructing my particular readings, I use the interchangeable expressions *logogic site* and *logogic crux*, by which I mean a whole text or one or more specific words in a text that provide a place for hesitation and contemplation. Whether the conscious construction of the author of the text or the unconscious expression of the author's reliance on cultural inheritance, the logogic site is a place where the pausing reader may sense the confluence of secular and divine meanings. This junction of temporal and eternal contexts derives authority, as Augustine insisted, from the Incarnation of the Logos (Word), who as Christ reaffirmed the union of matter and spirit in humanity as well as the bond between the order of nature and that of heaven. The logogic cruxes of Puritan American literature evidence a Christlike intersection of historical connotation and allegorical denotation.

My sense of the Puritan logogic crux is in some major respects similar to the concept of *les lieux de mémoire* advanced by the French historian Pierre Nora.[3] In contrast to the historian's usual preoccupation with *realia*, things in themselves, Nora emphasizes *les lieux de mémoire*. These sites of memory close in upon themselves as signs and at the same time always open to potential signification. Given this dualism, Nora indicates, these sites—as strategic, representational highlights—negotiate the gap between memory (spontaneous and intimate remembrance within the sacred) and history (analytical and distant recollection within the secular). *Les lieux de mémoire* combine eternity and time, the sacred and the profane, the collective and the individual, as if they were Möbius strips continually recycling past meanings and proliferating new ramifications. In this complex amalgamation of the material and the spiritual, the literal and the symbolic, *les lieux de mémoire* perform very similarly to the logogic sites of Puritan American authors.

When these authors were aware of these sites in their own work, they believed they had discovered and disclosed them rather than invented them. We might suspect otherwise, but from the Puritan American writer's point of view, words are like the details of nature: expressions or signs replete with divine signification. These natural signs were considered to be as determined in definition as were biblical types, which were closed in their meanings and, as Samuel Mather characteristically warned, should not be subjected to fanciful applications.[4] Nevertheless, in their Augustinian heritage Puritan American authors found authority to "play," if reverently and guardedly, with natural and verbal signs, and in the process, from our perspective at least, they indeed fashioned art.

From their perspective human art was altogether likely to manifest artfulness, a form of corrupt craftiness revealing pride, even a form of iconic idolatry of the self. The human artistic artifact, they thought, always threatened to become a false god or a Tower of Babel. As a result, they preferred to intertwine their contaminated artistry with the scriptural revelations of divine design, the only true art. This desire is particularly evident at the logogic sites in their writings. The logogic crux provided a most appealing opportunity for them because its very nature depended on the subtle intersection of the artist's temporal meanings and of the Creator's divine definitions.

The more complex and convoluted this interweaving of the artist's craft and the Creator's artistry at these sites, the more the Puritan American writer could mediate authorial anxiety through his or her own art. At this intersection of the divine and the material at the logogic crux the Puritan American writer tried to displace pride in his or her potentially idolatrous act of personal expression with a hope concerning his or her own spiritual fate. In effect, celebrating the Incarnation at the logogic site was a means for the artist to suspend both despair and presumption, the two extreme responses of the soul. The logogic crux mediated despair over any evidence of damning authorial pride in the Puritan artist's artful ingenuity and presumption over any evidence of humble authorial service in his or her divinely assisted artistic revelations of God's concealed aesthetic design. As a result, logogic cruxes were places for the reader—and in every case the author was the first reader of his or her own work—to hesitate and contemplate the duality of signification in the temporal world.

The works I have chosen for discussion comprise an arbitrary assemblage. In one sense, they are arbitrarily selected insofar as they represent authors from a single geographic region of the New World. In another sense, they are arbitrarily associated insofar as the geographic and the theological background of their authors allows us to designate their writings as American and as Puritan. Although my discussion is designed to explore one major feature of Puritan writers who settled in the New World, it makes no claim for the exclusivity of this feature or for its particularly American nature. In some form, the logogic crux may also be a characteristic of sixteenth-century or seventeenth-century European Puritan literature. Since the early New England colonists were primarily English citizens, my consideration of their writings deliberately leaves open the question of just what does constitute the identity of American literature and American literary tradition.[5]

My assembly of works in this study is arbitrary in a still more obvious sense. Like a journeyer whose travel has been extensive but whose later account of it highlights only those moments that in retrospect matter most, I have settled for a chosen few Puritan American texts for my discussion: an account of Plymouth colony by William Bradford, a polemic by Thomas Morton, a comment on art by Richard Mather, a dramatization of Satan and a meditation by Edward Taylor, a poetic autumnal reflection by Anne Bradstreet, a satire by Nathaniel Ward, an elegy by Urian Oakes, and a few early sermons by Jonathan Edwards. With a glance toward the future, I consider an eighteenth-century allegory of sorts by Nathan Fiske and a late nineteenth-century short story by Edward Bellamy as two works that draw upon their Puritan heritage yet radically mutate the Puritan American logogic site. I could have selected other works, but I preferred these writings initially because for some reason I enjoyed them more than others and found myself especially reflecting over them. Loitering at these sites individually eventually gave way to an exploration of the curious connections between these writings. After a while, it was difficult for me to think of some of these works without an awareness of the reinforcing or dialogic mates with which they had become associated in my mind. I can only hope that some of my readers will grant me this liberty and perhaps finally benefit from my particular pairings of texts, and the more general associations I note between all of them. And I can only hope that my effort to transmute these associations into literary critical metaphoric sites in my own commentary succeeds to some extent in revealing a concealed feature of Puritan American artistry.

Parts of this book appeared in earlier versions, often with a different focus, and are identified in the notes. Since the publication of these earlier explorations was a strong incentive to me professionally, I acknowledge my indebtedness to editors Herbert Brown, Emory Elliott, Everett Emerson, William M. Fowler, Jr., Harrison T. Meserole, Jean Pfaelzer, Charles L. Proudfit, Jean-Robert Rougé, Michael Schuldiner, and J. Edwin Whitesell. As a fellow editor, I know about the nature of their enterprise. And Philip Gura, University of North Carolina at Chapel Hill, generously advised me on Nathan Fiske.

I am especially grateful to Catherine Rainwater, who unselfishly surrendered precious time from her scholarly pursuits in order to attend to my effort here. "The best mirror is an old friend" (George Herbert).

1

The Necessity of Language

Sometimes the best laid schemes of the best of men and women do indeed go astray, and badly. This was certainly the opinion of William Bradford as he pondered in his later years the condition of the Pilgrims in Plymouth colony. It was, as well, the opinion of Thomas Morton as he fretted over the destruction of his settlement, and of Richard Mather as he considered ministerial responsibilities in his mission to make a clearing in the New World wilderness. And it was also the opinion of Edward Taylor as he reflected on the effect of Satan's scheming on humanity's experiences and on Satan's own diabolical aims. For all of these authors, whether by accident or by design, human langage served as a central component in the dilemma each of them contemplated.

Words Like Wooden Horses
William Bradford and Thomas Morton

When Bradford wrote in a letter to the Council of New England about the "many necessities . . . undergone, incident to the raw and immature beginnings of such great exertions," he was describing the Pilgrim undertaking as he saw it on 28 June 1625.[1] If he ever reread this letter in his old age, or recollected it, he probably would have done so with a sense of irony. For by then in his mind the word *necessity* had developed quite a history in the course of the Pilgrim enterprise.

In Bradford's *Of Plymouth Plantation* the word *necessity*

initially refers to the inability of humanity to master itself or its world. Humanity, according to Pilgrim belief, is directed by forces outside its control and its immediate comprehension. These forces may be manifest in the internal disposition of one's self or in the external eventuation of natural occurrences, but in both instances they are always divinely predestined. Necessity is, the Pilgrims maintained, the divinely sanctioned law of the postlapsarian world.

"A man's way is not in his own power, God can make the weak to stand," Bradford writes, "Let him also that standeth take heed lest he fall."[2] This was the lesson taught, for example, by the death of the profane sailor, whose end was more painful than any of the illnesses suffered by the voyaging Pilgrims at whom he swore (p. 59); and it was the lesson taught by the vexing of John Peirce, who had cheated the Pilgrim colony but was "marvelously crossed" by God (p. 124). These episodes are typical of a pattern in Bradford's history, in which time and again utter necessity coerces the colony to rely on divine providence.

Given this emphasis, it is not surprising that one might remark "an air of inevitability" in this document, as if "it is history itself that addresses the reader through the passive, accurate, self-effacing narrator."[3] And this emphasis augments the architectural shape of the narrative: "the downward curve of failing strength, the reversal through recognition and submission, and the ascent which measures the force of God's sustaining hand."[4] Bradford is certain that the experience of painful necessities, by individuals and by the colony as a whole, represents a form of divine communication. The distress caused by an emergent necessity might temporarily obscure the fact that "the providence of God [is] working for their good beyond man's expectation" (p. 54); but, as Bradford states in his verse treatment of the famine experienced by the colonists, every such vexation finally communicates a fundamental lesson: "That we might learn on providence to wait."[5]

For Bradford providential necessity is a taxing, yet ultimately benign directive from God: "Whom [God] loves he doth chastise / *And then* all Tears wipes from their eyes,"

Bradford writes in a epitaph he composed for himself.[6] In *Of Plymouth Plantation* the Pilgrim migration from England, in order to reestablish the church in "primitive order, liberty and beauty" (p. 3), is necessitated by the persecution of divine truth and of those who seek that truth. An explicit instance of the role of necessity in this migration surfaces in Bradford's discussion of the plight of the Scrooby congregation. The wives and the children of this group had been detained from joining their husbands and fathers in Amsterdam, and Bradford indicates how helpless everyone was in securing their release. Only the complexity of circumstances—the bad publicity the captors would earn and the inability of the women and the children to return to homes already sold—provides the solution. Concluding his account of these people Bradford observes: "Though in the meantime they (poor souls) endured misery enough; and thus in the end necessity forced a way for them" (p. 14).

The Pilgrims' sojourn in Holland is merely one stop in a much longer journey, something they discover as a result of the further pressure of necessity. Besides the difficulty many of them experienced in earning a living in Leyden, the physical and spiritual ills to which their children were now exposed, and their desire to herald the gospel in the New World, "it was not only probably thought, but apparently seen, that within a few years more they would be in danger to scatter, by necessities pressing them, or sink under their burdens, or both" (p. 24). In this instance, the threat of a bad necessity necessitates a preventive action by the Pilgrims. Reviewing the total Leyden experience, Bradford records the need of the colonists to make a change, "as necessity was a taskmaster over them" (p. 24).

Even in the New World, as Bradford's letter to the Council of New England indicates, the Pilgrims experience further instruction from this taskmaster. Necessity leads some colonists to steal corn and beans from Native Americans in 1620, and from the plantation itself in 1622 (pp. 66, 112). Typically, however, the hardship underlying these episodes yields a benign outcome that seemingly further reveals the divine scheme for the Pilgrims. In his entry for 1623, however, Bradford records a similar event with a subtle difference. This incident concerns the allocation of private property to members of the colony, a decisive moment that intimates a turning point in Bradford's perception of Pilgrim arguments based on necessity.

To appreciate this crux in Bradford's manuscript, his vision of the Pilgrim colony must be recalled. From the outset, as Bradford records, the Pilgrim spokesmen hoped to establish an ideal community. In Bradford's view, Plymouth colony corresponded to Israel, a correlation implying a special divine call to the Pilgrims to form an ideal community in the New World (p. 19).[7] This ideal community would, moreover, reenact the Pilgrims' sense of the communalism of the first generation of Christians. In this dual Old Testament and New Testament sense, Plymouth colony would transcend the merely superficial agreement, based on the Pilgrims' commercial indenture: to remain bound together for seven years, to place all profits in a general fund, and to cultivate common, not private, property (p. 40).[8] In this ideal community the individual self presumably would be renounced and would find proper identity from its participation in a sanctioned collective self.[9]

This utopian collective could fall short of its objective if even one member refused to submit to it, for "one wicked person may infect many" (p. 321). And, as Bradford's account indicates, the two chief affronts to the Pilgrim community did indeed derive from a few rebellious individuals swollen with pride and ambition (p. 4).[10] "So uncertain are the mutable things of this unstable world," Bradford muses, "and yet men set their hearts upon them, though they daily see the vanity thereof" (p. 119). From the beginning to the end of Bradford's narrative the Pilgrims are surrounded by people corrupted by pride and ambition: for example, Captain Reynolds, master of the lesser of the two ships contracted to sail to the New World, cheats them because of his "self-love" (p. 54); the Narragansetts threaten war as a result of "their own ambition" to dominate weaker Native Americans (p. 96); the Adventurers "over pride themselves" in the *Little James*, which subsequently has no success (p. 139); and Isaac Allerton, who eventually "gat little good, but went by the loss by God's just hand," falls prey to his ambition for wealth (p. 245).

Whatever such external threats to the colony, however, the

worst perils emerge from within the colony itself whenever the prideful ambition of its members erupts. Returning to the episode Bradford recorded for the year 1623, we can assess this problem specifically in terms of his emphasis on necessity. In this year, Bradford reports, a dispute over the cultivation of private land arose among the colonists, and the Pilgrim leaders, specifically Bradford as governor, found it necessary to portion land to individual families. This action violated the Pilgrim ideal of early Christian communalism as well as their commercial contract, but it was taken as a practical means to motivate people who balked at working only for the collective benefit of the group to "raise as much corn as they could, and obtain a better crop than they had done." Bradford writes: "The experience that was had in this common course and condition, tried sundry years and that amongst godly and sober men, may well evince the vanity of that conceit of Plato's and other ancients applauded by some of later times; that the taking away of property and bringing in community into a commonwealth would make them happy and flourishing; as if they were wiser than God. For this community (so far as it was) was found to breed much confusion and discontent" (pp. 120-21). On the surface Bradford's comment seems to suggest that this episode in the Pilgrims' experience was one more example of providential necessity at work as a divine taskmaster. And perhaps it is understandable that this passage has been read as an unequivocal assertion of Bradford's belief in private property.[11] Nevertheless, a sensitivity to Bradford's use of language in this passage suggests a different perspective on private property and, as well, exposes the sort of crux Pilgrims and Puritans found to be endemic to postlapsarian human language.

Does not Bradford's qualification evident in the phrase "and that amongst godly and sober men" betray a certain reluctance to write of the matter on his own authority? Is not a similar hesitation suggested in his comment that "the Governor (with the advice of the chiefest amongst them) gave way that they should set corn every man for his own particular" (p. 120)? And in this instance is not Bradford's own authority both diffused

The Necessity of Language 11

among the "chiefest amongst them" and in some sense compromised by the expression "gave way"? More is involved here than conscious defensiveness over the restrictions of the seven-year commercial contract denying such individual cultivation of land. Bradford, the governor, has given way as well to the end of the Pilgrim ideal of a Christian commonwealth, a meaning not successfully disguised by his attribution of that ideal to pagan Plato. Nor does his rationalization finalizing his account of this incident fully erase his hesitation: "Let none object this is man's corruption, and nothing to the course itself. I answer, seeing all have this corruption in them, God in His wisdom saw another course fitter for them" (p. 121). Bradford's admission that corruption is indeed involved outweighs his transference of the decision "to give way" to the divine taskmaster of divine necessity. The words "gave way" intimate not only Bradford's unconscious sense that this decision may presage the imminent failure of the Pilgrim mission but also, as we shall see, an eventual shift in Bradford's sense of the reliability of human interpretations of such logogic sites as the word *necessity*.

At the secular level this decision to grant private property at first appears to produce good results: "the effect of their particular planting was well seen, for all had, one way and other, pretty well to bring the year about; and some of the abler sort and more industrious had to spare, and sell to others" (p. 132). Four years later, however, land re-emerges as a critical issue, and once again the colony must accommodate human ambition (p. 188). Increasingly in *Of Plymouth Plantation* the necessity requiring the land decision of 1623 appears to have operated less as a divine directive designed to reduce prideful humanity to submission before God, than as a corrupt human justification to indulge human pride and ambition.

It is doubtful that Bradford quite realized in the 1640s, while penning the entry for 1623, that his sense of the nature of necessity was now in transition. Eventually, as scholars agree, he did indeed recognize that the colony was in decline, its mission unfulfilled, its purpose apparently abandoned by divine providence.[12] Even in the entry for 1623, however, Bradford intuitively hints at what he would directly articulate in his commentary on 1632: that the land decision marked the dissolution of the communal ideal in Plymouth and, as well, the apparent end of its special covenant with God. In 1638, when some members of the colony contemplate leaving in order to obtain still more private property, an earthquake occurs, "as if the Lord would hereby show the signs of His displeasure, in their shaking a-pieces and removals one from another" (p. 302). For several years after that incident, Bradford notes, Plymouth experienced cool summers and untimely frosts that adversely affected the colonists' harvests.

In the years between 1623 and 1632, it seemed to Bradford, necessity still operated in favor of the Pilgrims. The disruptive difficulties generated by the presence of John Lyford and John Oldham yielded good results insofar as "these troubles produced a quite contrary effect, in sundry here, than these adversaries hoped for. Which was looked at as a great work of God, to draw on men by unlikely means, and that in reason might rather have set them further off" (p. 164). Similarly, when necessity deprived the colonists of two leaders, a reminder of their utter dependence upon providence, "the lord so helped them . . . as now when they were at lowest they began to rise again, and being stripped in a manner of all human helps and hopes, He brought things about otherwise, in His divine providence" (p. 181). In retrospect, all of these signs would prove a deception to Bradford's interpretative eye.

In his entry for 1632, Bradford begins to confront the possibility that his previous reading of necessity was mistaken, particularly concerning the land decision of 1623. He now begins to suspect that arguments based on the word *necessity* may have been only a justification of the fallen necessities, the prideful proclivities, of depraved human desires rather than a valid interpretation of divine mandate. Had he unwittingly accommodated human ambition? Trying to read the signs, he now had cause to ponder the logogic site provided by the word *necessity*, especially since the rationale for the relentless changes corrupting the colony's ideal was specifically expressed in necessitarian terms.

In the entry for 1632, Bradford registers concern over the possibility that the prosperity resulting from his land decision of 1623 is a more vexed matter than he had previously suspected.[13] "And yet in other regards this benefit turned to their hurt, and this accession of strength to their weakness," Bradford observes, "for now as their stocks increased and the increase vendible, there was no longer any holding them together, but now they must *of necessity* go to their great lots" (p. 253; emphasis added). By echoing their use of the word *necessity* in their justification, Bradford registers a hint of irony. He now perceives that the word *necessity,* so prevalent in the Pilgrims' intial reading of their mission (as recorded in Bradford's history), is being invoked not to define divine intention but to defend human ambition. Surely Bradford was among those who countered the argument of the people who wished to depart from the colony and who concluded about these people that "it was not for want or necessity so much that they removed as for the enrichment of themselves" (p. 333).

From this point on in the history Bradford's use of the word *necessity* takes a different course. It now defines human motive, not divine intent, as Bradford records the supplanting of the pious Pilgrim mission by pride, leading to the division of the church and the betrayal of the Christian communal ideal in Plymouth. He specifically remarks that the colonists' perverse reading of divine intention—"thinking their own conceived necessity . . . a warrant sufficient for them"—will "be the ruin of New England, at least of the churches of God there, and will provoke the Lord's displeasure against them" (p. 254).

Bradford notes that other areas of New England have also succumbed to human ambition through similarly deceptive arguments based on necessity. In defending their immigration to Connecticut, for example, the Dorchester congregation explains that it is "well known that they are upon a barren place, where they were by necessity cast; and neither they nor theirs could long continue upon the same" (p. 283). Of the controversy between them and Massachusetts Bay, Bradford notes in his understated manner: "the controversy ended but the unkindness not so soon forgotten" (p. 284). In Bradford's opinion, the Christian communal ideal, imaged by him as a closely knit family, has vanished. Particularly in Plymouth "this poor church [was] left, like an ancient mother grown old and forsaken by her children . . . these of later time being like children translated into other families" (p. 334).[14]

Bradford remained certain that necessity governed the postlapsarian world, but he came to understand that human insight into this taxing yet ultimately beneficent taskmaster goading one to actions in conformity to the scheme of divine providence was much harder to read, to interpret, than he had initially thought. As his narrative shifted from a public record to a private document and as his consciousness of the unfathomableness of human existence deepened in the face of the ambiguous complexity of the historical world and of human behavior,[15] the word *necessity* became for Bradford a dreadful crux of nettlesome uncertainty, one of "the mutable things of this unstable world."

One of the final entries in his manuscript testifies to Bradford's eventual awareness of how destabilized his interpretation of the word *necessity* had become. In old age he apparently reread a letter he had included by John Robinson and William Brewster in an early part of the history. The passage on which he focused reads: "We are knit together as a body in a most strict and sacred bond and covenant of the Lord" (p. 33). On the blank page opposite this entry Bradford sadly made his final comment on Pilgrim arguments based on necessity: "O sacred bond, whilst inviolab[l]y preserved! . . . But (alas) that subtle serpent hath slyly wound in himself under the fair *pretenses of necessity* and the like, to untwist these sacred bonds" (p. 33; emphasis added). Necessitarian arguments, like any other justification necessarily expressed in human language, might be a direct reflection of divine providence or might be a twisted Satanic version of that providence.

Bradford could no longer attribute one certain meaning to the word *necessity*. Initially he had understood the word to signify the divine management of the external world as a relatively clear directive to the Plymouth colonists; now he understood that these colonists (and he himself in 1623) had used that word not to describe providential goals but to accommodate the prideful ambitions of the innately depraved human heart. As an interpreter he was now stymied by an unstable logogic crux comprised of two opposing possible readings. The temporal and the divine intersected at this logogic site, but he could not untangle them to read divine meaning.

Of course, in Bradford's opinion, even perverse necessitarian arguments ultimately served providential necessitarian design; but he himself, as historian, could no longer decode the role of Plymouth colony or of himself in this denotative divine scheme. What once seemed clear was now obscure to his understanding. His interpretative vision thus occluded, one feature of his waning vision of the Pilgrim experiment, Bradford contemplatively hesitated over the logogic crux of *necessity* in his addendum. Perhaps in his old age (and possibly with diminished eyesight) he concluded with more conviction than ever before that "God's judgments are unsearchable" and that one must be circumspect in being "bold with God's judgments" (pp. 177, 290).

Can the entire colonial enterprise of the Pilgrims be summed up in a single word? Of course not, but the word *necessity* in *Of Plymouth Plantation* opens a metonymic window not only to Bradford's view of what happened to his colony but also for our perception of an abiding Pilgrim/Puritan problem with language. Language was itself a necessity, but a nettlesome one replete with so many connotations of indeterminate denotative meaning that human interpretations remained fundamentally destabilized.

The capacity of words to appear to signify one thing and also subtly to signify something antithetical—Bradford's disconcerting discovery about *necessity*—is (ironically, one might observe) suggested in Thomas Morton's *New English Canaan* (1637). This satire on the Pilgrims' interpretation of reality can be critically approached as a gloss on Bradford's plight in *Of Plymouth Plantation*. Morton first arrived in New England in the Spring of 1624[16] and possibly heard something of Bradford's rationale for the land decision of 1623. Curiously in *New*

English Canaan Morton seizes upon the ideal of the Platonic commonwealth—specifically cited by Bradford as impossible to attain—and applies it to the Native Americans, whose humanity Morton consistently contrasts with the inhumanity of the Pilgrims:[17] "They love not to bee cumbered with many utensilles, and although every proprietor knowes his owne, yet all things (so long as they will last), are used in common amongst them. . . . Platoes Commonwealth is so much practised by these people."[18]

Such barbed, direct satire certainly evidences the power of language, but the capacity of words to contain more than they seem to say, a hidden power, is also suggested in another development of Morton's management of his theme of the inhumanity of the Pilgrims and the humanity of the Native Americans. This latent capacity lies concealed within Morton's allusion to the Trojan horse in his book.

Morton reports an incident concerning the desecration of a Native American "monument of the ded at Pasonayessit," the erection of which struck the Pilgrims as "an act of superstition" (pp. 106, 51). Enraged, the Native Americans seek "revenge of those uild people," but they are routed by the saints (p. 107). This event is repeated at Merry Mount, where the maypole, another monument, is destroyed by the Separatist barbarians. According to Morton, the maypole was part of a celebration planned for "the festivall day of Philip and Iacob," and was to be held "in a solemne manner with Revels, & merriment after the old English custome" (p. 132). Both points suggest that this celebration was only an observation of a tradition of civilization. To the ignorant Pilgrims, however, the maypole is a superstitious "Idoll," and they cut it down and destroy the settlement (p. 134).

These two parallel episodes in which uncivilized forces victimize the representatives of civilized behavior are redressed by the hint in Book III that both acts will eventually be avenged. Morton indicates early in this last section of his book, for instance, that "Hanniball when hee had to doe with Fabius, was kept in awe more by the patience of that one enemy, then by the resolution of the whole army: A well tempered enemy is

The Necessity of Language 17

a terrible enemy to incounter" (p. 119). In other words, Morton will abide his time patiently, a sinister point reinforced by his subsequent allusion to the Trojan horse.

This allusion occurs in the scene in which the Pilgrim soldiers become inebriated in celebration of their victory over Merry Mount: "The Conspirators sported themselves at my honest host, that meant them no hurt; & were so joccund that they feasted their bodies, and fell to tippeling, as if they had obtained a great prize; like the Trojans when they had the custody of Hippeus pinetree horse" (p. 139). The great prize is the maypole, a "goodly pine tree of 80. foote longe" (p. 132). The word "pine" connects the Trojan horse and the maypole, and intimates that the Pilgrims' and Puritans' prize will eventually lead to their undoing.

Appropriately, *New English Canaan* concludes in the voice of Jonah speaking from the belly of the whale, that is, from the hold of the ship serving Morton as a surrogate image for the wooden horse: "And now mine Host being merrily disposed, haveing past many perillous adventures in that desperat Whales belly, beganne in a posture like Ionas, and cryed Repent you cruell Seperatists repent, there are as yet but 40. dayes if Iove vouchsafe to thunder, Charter and the Kingdome of the Seperatists will fall a sunder" (p. 188). Morton is within the belly of the whale (ship), just as the Greeks were inside the belly of the Trojan horse, and his weapon is the book he is writing. Morton presents himself, as Daniel B. Shea has observed, as a Proteus figure who re-creates himself and recovers the land from which he has been banished by means of the regenerative power of textual nomination (naming) in *New English Canaan*.[19] Just as Morton shall emerge from the pine trophy of the ship, so shall the words from his book, which in fact played a part in his attempt with Archbishop William Laud, during the 1630s, to nullify the Massachusetts Bay Company patent. By appealing to the English king (Jove) to revoke this charter, the words of Morton's book threaten his enemies with the same destruction the Pilgrims have wrought on the Native Americans and on Merry Mount, with the same plight that befell Troy.

The potential for this revenge lies concealed in his words, just as the threat he is making lies hidden in his subtle management of the allusion to the Trojan horse in *New English Canaan*. The capacity for human language to evince a subtle duplicity, an interior destabilization of its apparent surface signification, and thereby to (from within) wreak havoc on a human community, is readily recognized by Morton. It is precisely this lesson that Bradford eventually learns concerning the word *necessity*.

Perhaps the pairing of Bradford and Morton in this way is arbitrary. But the coupling of these two old antagonists yields a fascinating curiosity; for if Morton's wooden-horse text did not eventuate in the nullification of the Massachusetts Bay charter, it did prophesy, in an apt image, the self-destruction of the Pilgrims (in Bradford's view) through the wooden-horse nature of human language. For Bradford the word *necessity* had amounted to nothing less than a Trojan horse. Morton could mediate this capacity of language, whereas Bradford could not. Morton was comfortable with his Renaissance inheritance of the genius and play of language. He almost instinctively fashioned the incantatory rhyming of "thunder" and "sunder" in his Jonah-like prediction, and he readily engaged in riddles in *New English Canaan*, not only overtly in "Rise Oedipus"[20] but also covertly in such allusions as the one to the Trojan horse. Mixing hyperbolic play and dire forecast, Morton comfortably assumed the persona of a voluble prophet at the end of his book. In contrast, Bradford preferred "a plain style, with singular regard unto the simple truth in all things" (p. 3). He winced before lingual ambiguity, and when confronted with it he fell into unprophetic silence at the end of his book on Plymouth plantation. For Pilgrims and Puritans alike, the nature of postlapsarian language, so referentially unstable before their interpretative eye, was the source of enormous tension and ambivalence. Some Puritan authors, however, would exploit this ambiguity and ambivalence consciously to create art.

Double-Talk
Renaissance and Reformed Traditions

For Bradford, finally, postlapsarian human language is coiled, similar to temporal history. As Bradford's marginalia on *necessity* indicates, a straightforward divine meaning underlies all temporal words and events, a signification that will be disclosed, or unfolded, at the Second Coming; but in the meantime, humanity struggles with the subtle sinuous ambiguities of Satanic influence in the world and in the human word. Pilgrims and Puritans alike pondered this mystery of human language, especially its ability to be used as an instrument of divine wisdom or as an instrument of Satanic sophistry.

Perry Miller, whose groundbreaking work on colonial America has been subjected to more abuse recently than is warranted,[21] has indicated the degree to which the Puritans studied logic, grammar, and rhetoric, with a special emphasis on the last as the primary mode of discourse concerned with communication. Miller reasonably concludes, "the Puritans, speaking as humanists, would be bound to exemplify in their theory of rhetoric a great love for it along with a nervous apprehension lest it be abused or over-worked."[22] In other words, while the Puritans believed in the ultimate denotative definitions of all language from the deity's point of view, they doubted the capacity of fallen human reason to escape the convoluted muddle of connotative meanings in the temporal world.[23] In this sense, the Puritans were at once the descendants of the Renaissance and the descendants of the Reformation.

In terms of their Renaissance heritage, the Puritans considered the power and beauty of language to be signs of the specialness of humanity in the natural scheme, at least before the Fall. Postlapsarian language might be used for good or for ill, for the Renaissance heritage in this instance was a dual one; and it was dual in a still more important sense as well. The Puritans' Renaissance heritage evidenced an encounter with two notions about the authorization of human language. On the one hand, a historicist impulse in this tradition emphasized the self-originated craftsmanship of the writer; on the other hand, an allegorical impulse in this tradition emphasized the deity-originated metaphysical truth disclosed by the writer. In the first instance, the authority of a text was assessed from within on the secular basis of its historical individuality, its difference from previous models of various meanings; in the second instance, the authority of the text was assessed from without on the metaphysical basis of its conformity, its similarity to previous canonical disclosures of divine meaning.

These two impulses conduct something of a dialogue in Renaissance writings, but finally the historicist impulse, with its stress on ideal texts as reflectors of individualistic human creative potentiality, tended to dominate the allegorical impulse, with its stress on ideal texts as reflectors of transcendent, revealed truth.[24] Primarily language was prized for its potentiality for good, especially the goodness of individual creativity. Whether used in celebratory art or in argumentative discourse, language was seen in the Renaissance as a discloser of the wondrous dimensions of the human mind.

Puritans inherited from their Renaissance predecessors this belief in language as an expression of the mind, or soul, which (in Puritan thought) bore the image of God. Moreover, for the Puritans, Christ and Scripture further indicated the sanctity of human language. Rhetoric in particular, the Puritans learned from Augustine and Renaissance authors (both tutored by the classics), is a divinely decreed means of forging order within the social bond.[25] Specifically, the ability to fashion a work of art represents the ability of humanity to fashion the protean self (such as it was understood at the time) into various modes of expression in the world.

In the Reformation heritage, which was as dualistic on the nature of language as was the Renaissance heritage, this protean self was treated with much more suspicion. In a sense, the Reformation can be read as a corrective to the eventual shift of the Renaissance toward the valorization of the individuality of the self and its artifacts; for one key element of the early Reformation, despite its own grounding on an individualistic break from the central authority of the Roman Catholic church, was the assault on the intrinsic nobility of the individual before God. This attitude toward the self included an assault on the intrinsic authority of human language, which Reformation tradition considered as Bablic whenever it corruptly claimed autonomy and self-authority.

In this sense, the Reformation recovered the allegorical impulse, which had eventually lost primacy in the secular world of the Renaissance. At the same time, the Reformation, itself an anxious expression of autonomous impulse, did not abandon the Renaissance regard for historical context,[26] with its valorization of human language. The Reformation was as dualistic as was the Renaissance concerning these two perceptions. In Reformed thought, however, the secular prioritization of historicist over allegorical reading was reversed, and language was principally valued as a revealer of transcendent truth rather than as a revealer of personal creativity.

Defined in terms of such doctrines as predestination and innate depravity, personal creativity was hardly as protean as suggested by Renaissance tradition. The Puritans in particular were sensitive to the capacity of the self to misuse language; then it would manifest the pride of its user and could deceive both the author and the audience. The Puritans had in mind more than their perception of the casuistry of Roman Catholic theologians, who they thought intentionally deceived their hearers. Their complaints against the papist Anglicans, specifically the Laudians, included carnal eloquence and ornateness, which they thought concealed unintentional ministerial pride and also inadvertently distracted the laity from the message of the sermons.

But the problem of postlapsarian language ran even deeper for the Puritans. With the Fall in Eden, in Reformed thought as influenced by Augustine, the human mind lost *sapientia*, a form of intuitive wisdom whereby Adam intrinsically knew the names (meanings) of things. After the Fall the human mind possesses only *scientia*, a good Adamic feature, but a capacity hierarchically lower than *sapientia*. *Scientia* is capable only of sensorial knowing, which leaves post-Adamic humanity dependent upon the deceptive senses for determining meanings.[27] Without grace, which restores something of *sapiential* knowing, humanity finds naming, the use of language, subject to confusion. This experience of obscured denotative signification, of language failing to close with its divine referent,[28] is a characteristic of fallen humanity. Nevertheless, in Reformed thought, all language does indeed have a final denotative referent in the divine mind. This ultimate signification exists as if it were a secret hidden within human discourse, just as definitive providential design lies within human history and within all of nature. Speaking in 1686 of creation (a plentitude including nature, history, and language), Samuel Danforth II typically points to this ultimate denotative signification; "Theyr Maker made them *signs*," and humanity "may *know*" in a "poor sense" "*What 'tis they signify.*"[29]

The Puritan inheritance of Reformed thought concerning language, at once an index to human corruption and to divine truth, included Augustine's profoundly influential sense of the nature of words. Augustine specifies the dual capacity of human discourse to be transitory when oriented toward selfish aims or to be eternal when serving as a medium of truth deepening both the author's and his or her audience's knowledge of divine reality. Augustine warns against an idolatrous worship of any sign, including the word, as an iconic graven image displacing its true source of signification: "Woe to those who love not you [God], but the signs you show, and who forget your meaning!"[30] Augustine, however, specifically points to the Incarnation of the Word of God as the coda for reading such signs, a coda that particularly restores authorization for the value of human words. For Augustine, such proper speech, influenced by the Holy Spirit, bridges the gap between the material and heavenly orders and partially, if truly, serves author and audience alike as a necessary and adequate means of contemplating God.[31]

So the Puritan inheritance of Reformed doctrine, which tended to emphasize somewhat the artful capacity of postlapsarian human language for disorder, did not simply displace the tendency of the Renaissance heritage to emphasize somewhat the artistic capacity of this language for order. Both of these traditions were dualistic on the subject of language, and a similar dualism survived in Puritan thought. Negotiating the countercurrents between these two heritages was the Puritan reliance upon Augustinian authority concerning postlapsarian language. As a result, they were certain that even if humans were fallible in decoding the ultimate divine meaning behind postlapsarian human language, that ultimate meaning nonetheless exists and endows language with a potentiality to serve as a divine instrument, as in ministerial discourse.[32] Pertinently, Edward Taylor, who believes "Words . . . by my Fall were spoild" ("Meditation 1.7"), also maintains that "Words and their Sense within thy bounds are kept" ("Meditation 2.106").[33] Taylor's indication that the denotative meanings of all human language reside within the Logos is not unique to him among Puritan authors. He states, in Augustinian terms, the essential fundamental Renaissance valuation of language that continued to prevail in some form within the more explicit Puritan Reformed skepticism over postlapsarian human language.[34]

Concealed Verbal Artistry
Richard Mather and Edward Taylor

Consider Richard Mather's practice, as reported by his son Increase: "His way of Preaching was plain. . . . Whence he studiously avoided obscure phrases, Exotick words, or an unnecessary citation of Latine Sentences, which some men addict themselves to the use of. . . . So did this humble man look upon the affectation of such things in a Popular Auditory to savour of Carnal wisdome. . . . He would often use that Saying, *Artis est celare Artem.*"[35] "This humble man"—and *humble* is the key word for Increase—wished to avoid the evidences of pride in his language. Human fashioning of language was not to be valued for itself any more than, as Increase demonstrates in his own artistic technique in this biography of his father,[36] Richard was to be valued for himself. Richard Mather wanted his language to conform to a received ideal, that "the function of art is to conceal art." The word *art* here becomes a logogic crux, its first appearance in the quotation (*Artis*) seeming to twist toward pronounced meaning, its second appearance (*Artem*) untwisting that promise, as if only paradox might somehow integrate the dual capacity of language to be both artful human craft and aesthetic divine design.

This ideal of concealed art is a Classical one often attributed to Horace. It is found in various guises throughout Renaissance writing and emerges in Ramistic thought and English Puritan discourse.[37] For a Puritan like Richard Mather, however, the word *art* becomes an ambiguous point of nervous mediation of the dual nature of language, as defined by both Renaissance and Reformed traditions. In his prefatory defense of the "plaine translation" attending "Conscience rather than Elegance, fidelity rather than poetry," in presenting "the Lords songs of prayse according to his owne will" in *The Bay Psalm Book* (1640),[38] Mather unknowingly echoes Bradford's preference for "a plain style, with singular regard unto the simple truth in all things." Mather's Renaissance and Reformed heritages taught him that human language is potentially either a divinely authorized artistic container of concealed pristine truth or a humanly authorized artful container of concealed corrupt authorial pride. Mather strove for an ideal mediation of human language similar to his appreciation of David's achievement in the Psalms: an artistic refinement (suppression and concealment) of opaque connotative meanings (*sciential* perception) to reveal (*sapiential* perception) a latent transparent (eternal) denotation. Such mediation, or possible conflation, of antithetical meanings within the word *art* in this instance recalls Bradford's sense of the duality of reference within the word *necessity*, and both logogic sites support Perry Miller's observation that the Puritans nervously combined a humanist affection for rhetoric (the expressive component of language) with a fear of its excess.

Precisely this coalescence of eternal truth and temporal deceit in words is highlighted in Edward Taylor's *Gods Determinations*. In this long poem Satan's speech represents the nature of all postlapsarian human language as a crux where duality of meanings must be negotiated. Intended for an audience and organized along the instructional Ramist principle of dichotomization,[39] *Gods Determinations* dramatizes Christ as the manifestation of divine mercy (the gospel) and Satan as the manifestation of divine justice (the law). Both are consummate rhetoricians, but whereas Christ speaks transparently in eternal denotative terms (the Covenant of Grace transcending time), Satan speaks opaquely in temporal connotative terms (the Covenant of Works defined by time). But just as Bradford's understanding of *necessity* and Mather's sense of *art* evidence the fusing of divine and demonic meanings, in Taylor's poem the rhetoric of Christ and of Satan intertwine, dialectically twisting and untwisting their respective meanings until the Second Coming.

For instance, *Gods Determinations* begins with an image of God's hands engaged in the act of creation, and throughout the following verses the salvation of the elect is depicted as a re-creation whereby the Son "Doth with his hands hold, and uphold the same."[40] Christ, as Mercy, thus promises in the case of every saint, "I'le make him hands of Faith to hold full fast" (p. 394). Without this assistance the elect would be helpless, as Satan reminds his hearers: "You'l then be mawld worse than the hand thats right / Between the heads of the Wheelhorn'd Rams that fight" (p. 404). The immediate context of Satan's comment about human hands is the postlapsarian condition of humanity as defined, as Satan says, in terms of "Natures Law: which Law he [God] Gave" (p. 424).

What Satan says is true, as far as it goes, and Satan is unwilling to go beyond the Covenant of Works, after the collapse of which humanity does indeed find itself with useless "iron hands" (p. 395). In this instance Satan emphasizes only one feature of the divine reality behind humanity's present circumstances: the wrathful aspect of divine Justice, before which humanity is utterly powerless. He prevaricates by omission; he makes no mention of the merciful side of the deity. In this way he distorts truth.

Nevertheless, always latently concealed and potentially detectable beneath the surface of his artful arguments are the transparent implications of the complete divine truth, which provides for a denotative alternative reading of his words. With the word *hand*, to continue our example, Satan further argues his case for interpreting experience in terms of the Covenant of Works, but he unwittingly also cues the elect to the underlying, denotative verity of the Covenant of Grace. Satan says, "God doth not Command / Such things of us as had are of no hand," and "Hence sprouts Presumption making much too bold / To catch such Shaddows which no hand can hold" (pp. 424, 425). These are true observations, but they can be used by the human hearer to despair or to hope, depending on whether one knows of only the first covenant or of both covenants. Whenever arguing from the Book of Nature, appealing to fallen reason through sensorial perceptions, or stressing the Law, Satan uses language that recalls Justice's indictment of humanity "for want of hands": "Whosoever trust doth to his golden deed / Doth rob a barren Garden for a Weed" (pp. 393, 396). In telling half the truth Satan conceals his art (a perverse sense of Mather's meaning) and distorts reality for the unwary.

This same focus on hands, however, potentially reminds the elect of the New Testament promise of faith and grace, of Christ's promise to "make [them] hands of Faith to hold full fast." The reader of Taylor's poem should pause over the logogic crux in Satan's references to hands, for they are images of concealed art. The imagery of hands craftily conveys dire implications when read in the light of the outmoded Covenant of Works stressed by Satan (Justice); and simultaneously this same imagery transparently conveys blessed implications when read in the light of the Covenant of Grace stressed by Christ (Mercy). Since the reader does not know whether he or she is saved or damned, the crux of unstable meaning in the word *hand* remains unresolved, a logogic site for ongoing (hopeful) contemplation concerning his or her spiritual state.

Regardless of his personal intentions and the apparent (surface) validity of what he says, Satan always intrinsically speaks the truth in some essential manner because the denotative reality of God defines everything in creation. This divine reference determinatively establishes an ineluctable context for every artful remark made by the devil in *Gods Determinations*. In the sermons of the *Christographia* Taylor clarifies this point when he explains that God "gives a permit to Satan . . . to bring forth his uttmost Diabolicall Subtilty into its highests, and magnificent exploits to Subvert, and overturn the Glorious Work of God in the Creation"; yet "the Wisdom of Divine Grace hath made the Old Serpents Wisdom a pen in the hands of his own Envy writing himselfe, whether he will or no, to be an Utter FOOLE," for "God makest his Design of Satans, destructive to Satans design and promoting of the whole Creation to a greater Glory."[41] Satan's language is a wooden horse, its intentional demonic art concealed from the unregenerate and its intrinsic divine art concealed from the devil himself. The hidden interior divine truth, rather than the hidden intent, of Satan's words will finally emerge to conquer both the unregenerate and their demonic author. Satan unavoidably serves as a divine agent and, ultimately for the elect, everything he says is informed by the eternal transparent denotation that Richard Mather indicated as the function of concealed verbal artistry. This concealed transparent art of God is eventually revealed from within Satan's effort to conceal his own artistry within his Trojan-horse language. Always detectable beneath the surface of his simplifying, selective (and hence twistedly distorted) rhetoric, as Taylor fashions it in the poem, is the complete divine truth. Whatever their superficial temporal connotative distortions for the unwary, Satan's words finally issue forth (as if from the belly of a Trojan horse) from within pristine divine meaning.

Satan's rhetoric in *Gods Determinations* principally deceives by depicting reality as an eternal dichotomy. His rhetoric is itself replete with dichotomization, and in effect paradoxically warns of the dual nature of the postlapsarian language he himself uses. He suggests that the sort of Manichean fissuring evident in the word *hand* (as in *necessity* for Bradford and in *art* for Mather) is cosmically stable. Satan seizes upon this notion because, as the author of sin, he mentally rebels against God, and through the perverse artistry of his confused mental state he derives an unstable connotative sense of things from natural law. Natural law seems to the sinner, human and demonic alike, to reflect irreconcilable warring factions. Satan's raison d'être in *Gods Determinations* arises from a distorted Manichean belief in such a permanent dichotomy in creation and in language. His sense of personal identity depends on the continued existence of creation caught between the forces of divine mercy (Christ) and divine justice (Satan). His unilateral emphasis on nature not only seemingly affirms this basis for his own existence; but, as a result of his position as a perverse mediator (anti-Christ) apparently inverting the order of creation, his emphasis on nature also represents his effort to increase the distance between God and humanity in order to widen commensurately the gap between himself and Christ. Satan's language of dichotomization seeks to define itself, give itself referential stability, by ever widening the alleged separation between the temporal and the eternal, both in terms of human experience and language. Satan's language relentlessly forces the unwary reader to interpret reality as a contest of immutable oppositions, of irresolvable dualistic meanings, interpretations, points of view.

In *Gods Determinations* Satan thrives on dichotomy, the cleavage between eternal denotative definitions and temporal connotative meanings. He has no other mode of existence. He asks, on the basis of connotative temporality, what can one do when the perceived forces of creation participate in an eternal contention and when all of humanity likewise is helplessly divided against itself? Satan's rhetoric of dichotomy, his double-talk, aims to recruit the beleaguered victim to his distorted views. Satan fears the restoration of the order of creation at the end of time, when his role as the agent of divine Justice will be revealed as merely the inversion of the mediatory role of Christ. Then his sense of personal identity, an illusion of self-defining referentiality in any event, will dissolve even as the appearance of an eternal dichotomy will disappear from postlapsarian creation. Then too, the denotative truth underlying his connotational distorted rhetoric will be revealed; then the Trojan-horse deception of his rhetoric will be made apparent: specifically that all of Satan's insistence on dichotomy has from within itself been latently in a concealed manner suggesting all along that there was another opposite version of his reading of creation. Then Satan's perception of cosmic dichotomy will be paradoxically shown to be false in its assertion of the pemanence of such a scheme and yet true in its underlying implication that God would indeed finally dialogically check such demonic half-truths as Satan artfully fashions.

Puritans like Taylor saw that postlapsarian human language is indeed double-talk, at once (to apply Bradford's metaphor) twisting (restricting) the temporal and untwisting (unfolding) the divine. The effort of Taylor's Satan to conceal the wile or craftiness of his rhetorical art in order to keep the fissure between eternal denotation and temporal connotation gaping wide and the aim of Richard Mather to conceal the cleverness of his rhetorical art in order to close this very gap, represent two instances of how Puritan art incorporated its dual Renaissance and Reformed heritage concerning language. In a sense, Taylor's Satan seeks to widen, whereas Mather tries to narrow, the interstice between the Puritan regard for and distrust of the verbal arts. As the representational moments of Bradford's hesitation over *necessity*, Mather's hesitation over *art*, and Taylor's hesitation over *hand* indicate, Puritan authors nervously approach postlapsarian human language with a keen awareness of its capacity for interweaving connotational ambiguities.

The negotiation of this problem of the unstable logogic crux is one brilliant feature of Puritan artistic practice. In the next chapter we will focus on two remarkable specific instances of this mediation, as Anne Bradstreet confronts the requirement "To sing some song" to "magnify" the "great Creator" but finds her lingual "imbecility" threatens to make her "mute"; and as Edward Taylor ponders an identical dilemma:

>   I fain would something say:
>   Lest Silence should indict me. Yet I feare
>   To say a Syllable lest at thy day
>   I be presented for my Tattling here.[42]

2

The Winding Sheet of Meditative Verse

A little more than fifty years have passed since Thomas H. Johnson first presented Edward Taylor's poetry to the public.[1] Since then, Taylor has emerged as the most outstanding poet of colonial America, even though his verse has remained obscure and enigmatic. Early commentary treated his poems collectively and primarily attempted to define the traditions informing them.[2] The *Preparatory Meditations* particularly tended to disturb Taylor's critics during the 1940s and 1950s, when various efforts were made to explain what seemed to some to be inept awkwardness or a Roman Catholic disposition in the poet's work. Even today a similar hesitation over propriety is occasionally registered in critical remarks on Taylor's work, and now and then one still encounters the unsupportable notion that because of the unorthodox nature of his verse, Taylor enjoined his heirs never to publish his writings. Many critics do not yet adequately appreciate the pluralism of Puritan culture or the intensity of Puritan sacramentality.[3]

Moreover, this search for informing traditions has often suggested in one way or another that Taylor's verse lacks something. The disparagement of Taylor's encounter with the emblem tradition, for example, is characteristic of this critical tendency. The two fullest treatments of this tradition in his verse find fatigue and chaos. One study concludes that Taylor's management of emblems demonstrates an exhaustion of a literary mode because in his poetry, which lacks tension, the poet refuses to grapple with his mind or his art.[4] The other study complains that Taylor employs a peculiar jumble of emblems in his meditations, that the poet mentions each emblem briefly only to abandon it as he moves on the next one.[5] Whenever the legitimate search for the traditions behind Taylor's poetry slips into such facile conclusions, possibly an unconscious critical agenda is intimated: a desire to explain away, rather than to explain, Taylor's poetry. This pattern of evasion, in my opinion, amounts to a profound shortcoming in Taylorian criticism during the last fifty years. In discussing Taylor's verse, most critics have simply preferred not to read, to decode, his poems. On the contrary, the critical interest in underlying traditions has led to generalizations, especially concerning the aesthetic attainment of his verse.

Even a recent, well-informed study of Taylor's use of typological tradition makes no case for the poetry. This study cites fragmentary moments when Taylor shows a "penchant for playfully manipulating words and images" or for forging "a striking imaginative adaptation" of a biblical type, but it readily concludes that Taylor is "a poet with limited skill, but glorious ambitions."[6] Similarly, another recent book calls for "close analysis" of Taylor's poems and for a particular sensitivity to how the poet develops derivative imagery "in his own imaginative context," but in fact this book evades both challenges in its discussion of the seventeenth-century tradition of humor. Concluding with a reference to Taylor's "evident faults as an artist," this study apologetically expresses doubt that the poet "would have left us better work had he spent all his days in Boston or London."[7]

With such conclusions so prevalent, it is not surprising that very few close readings of any Taylorian poem have been ventured. Longstanding has been the notion that the diverse data in a poem by Taylor defy organization, that the poet's method is one of random image-making.[8] Given such a critical tradition during the last fifty years, it was perhaps predictable that finally someone should justify the avoidance of close readings by bluntly dismissing the *Preparatory Meditations* as numbing and lacking in even one successful poem.[9]

Similarly, critics who bypass the issue of historical traditions and approach Taylor's verse in terms of some contemporary literary critical theory avoid approaching Taylor's poems as texts to be read. A representative recent instance offers a bare application of Paul Ricoeur's theory of metaphor and concludes that the disparity of Taylor's metaphors amounts to a semantic impertinence replacing the confusion of rational sense with a new predictive meaning, which reduces the distance between the poet and the deity.[10] This conclusion amounts to a restatement of early observations during the 1960s about Taylor's use of metaphor; but more pertinent here is its echo of the notion that his poems manifest an internal disorder. Such implicit indictments of aesthetic incoherence covertly defend the prevailing critical avoidance of approaching Taylor's poems individually as texts to be read.

Curiously, whether approached through the literary traditions of the past or through the critical lore of the present, Taylor's verse has in a sense been prematurely deconstructed. His poetry has never received the sort of close readings that canonical American writings, now under the hammers of deconstruction, have previously enjoyed. Consequently, if critics have seen Taylor's literary heritage, they have not seen his poetry, or the poet. Deconstruction of any kind is inherently premised on the sense that there is a text to de-compose, yet it is precisely Taylor's texts that have been ignored.

If Edward Taylor's poetry has on the whole not fared well in assessments of its aesthetic achievement, Anne Bradstreet's verse (which Taylor knew) has received still worse treatment. Much of what she has written, albeit of thematic interest to feminist scholars, represents modes of verse that are not much to literary taste today. "Contemplations" (written during the 1650s or 1660s) comes closest to being an exception to this disregard. "Contemplations" has generally been recognized as Bradstreet's best work, and it is routinely included in anthologies that print selections from her writings. Nevertheless, although "Contemplations" has been mined by literary critics for biographical traces of the poet's feelings and of her studies[11] and for its thematic continuities with her other poetry,[12] in fact it has been generally neglected as literary art.[13] This neglect is also particularly odd because scholars of early American culture are well aware of the importance of the emblem tradition in Puritan art, evident as well in Taylor's meditative verse; nevertheless, somehow these scholars avoid any serious closure with the fact that "Contemplations" specifically refers to emblems.[14]

A careful consideration of this poem, as we shall see, reveals that an emblem of the Christian cross lies artistically concealed beneath its surface. This emblem functions as a logogic site integrating theme, structure, and symbolism in the poem, with the result that "Contemplations" is not only Anne Bradstreet's most accomplished poem but also a very remarkable example of New England Puritan art. Bradstreet does not deserve to be dismissed as the author of merely "provincial verse, or doggerel," or as an author of mere historical interest, as the first published American colonial poet to whom "the homage due . . . has little to do with literary merit."[15]

Bradstreet's "Contemplations" and Taylor's *Preparatory Meditations* contain numerous authorially intentional signs, not only of literary traditions and of the inability of human language to signify something ultimate; they also convey signs of two poets who (at least from our perspective) find within these authorizing traditions and de-authorizing lingual limitations an opportunity for artistic innovation and originality. Nor, as we shall see, does their mutual inheritance of the emblem tradition deter their creativity.[16] On the contrary, both authors treat the poetic management of emblems as logogic cruxes, so that "Contemplations" and (typically for Taylor) "Meditation 1.19" are replete with the sort of double bind evident, as we saw in chapter 1, in Bradford's sense of the word *necessity*, Mather's sense of the word *art*, and Taylor's sense of the word *hand*.

Not only do I find Bradstreet and Taylor to be more inventive and poetically accomplished than does the critical consensus about their work, but I find the play of these qualities in their poetry to be coherent rather than chaotic. The intentional appearance of disorder in their verse strikes me as a disguise,[17] a contrived discord appropriate to the humble poet Bradstreet desires to be and to the inept poet Taylor appropriately pretends to be as they confront, in Bradford's phrase, "the mutable things of this unstable world." "Contemplations" and "Meditation 1.19" are remarkable examples of how Puritan authors practiced the idea, as summarized by Richard Mather, that the function of art is to conceal art.

Both poets hesitate before the unstable crux of language, before the intersection of temporal artful connotation and eternal artistic denotation in their verbal emblems. In this sense, they possess an abiding awareness of postlapsarian language as double-talk. Bradstreet and Taylor recognize the inadequacy of words, but both equally recognize the wonder of language, its sanction by the Logos, and the obligation of the soul to use it (albeit nervously) in meditative song. Behind Bradstreet's humble fracturing of her monument in verse and beneath Taylor's guise of surface disorder and (sometimes humorous) ineptitude is a poetic management of emblematic evidence of a real, divinely ordained cohesion and unity which, each poet hopes, is the divine denotative art concealed within their human Bablic artfulness. For both authors, possibly, glints of this aesthetic order at the integrative logogic site encouraged some precarious hope. Perhaps their awkward artistry seemed, to apply Morton's metaphor, like a Trojan horse concealing not a wrathful enemy (such as Satan indicates in *Gods Determinations*), but a merciful redeeming friend (such as Christ indicates in *Gods Determinations*).

Read in this way, the proliferation of imagery or the fracturing of structure or the distortion of syntax or the departure from convention is no index to any fundamental ineptitude or disorder in Bradstreet's or Taylor's poetry, but, instead, a clever covert (art-concealing) demonstration of fundamental denotative relationships. The detection (though we might see it as *invention*) of these radical relationships at the logogic sites of their verse, both poets suggest, is the product of the remotest recesses of their reason and will, the image of God in them. Presumably as they contemplate the logogic cruxes of their emblematic verse, they find a nervous hope in their possible election by God.

The Wrack of Mortal Poets
Anne Bradstreet's "Contemplations"

The theme of "Contemplations" is less the beauty of nature than the nature of time. As we shall see, the eternity of Eden is contrasted in the poem with life on earth, "A lonely place, with pleasures dignified" (line 144).[18] This theme is reinforced by the poet's emphasis on the role of pride in the loss of that eternal bliss, and in the need for humility if one is to benefit from temporal existence. These and other dialectical polarities comprise Anne Bradstreet's thematic concerns,[19] and they are particularly embodied in the structure and the symbolism of her poem.

That the structure of "Contemplations" has not attracted much critical interest[20] is surprising because the progression, or movement, of the poem draws attention to itself. The poem fractures in several places, falls into disjunctive gaps or lacunae. This fissuring occurs three times, thereby creating four discrete units within the work. These units include stanzas 1 to 9, 10 to 20, 21 to 28, and 29 to 33. Their identity as units of development and their sequential order are important to observe.

The First Movement. The first unit (stanzas 1 to 9) presents the poet in a natural setting. It is an evening in autumn, and as an adult (in the autumn, evening, stage of her life) the poet is appropriately contemplating. She contemplates nature, what the Puritans called the Book of Nature. Indeed the New England autumn leaves are so brilliantly colored they seem "painted" and "gilded o'er" (lines 4-5) as if they were a medieval illuminated manuscript. The Book of Nature is the art work of the Logos, the Word of God, and of course it surpasses any art work a human might create.

The poet specifically focuses on the trees within the wondrous art of the Logos in nature. The trees are "richly clad" and "stately" (lines 3, 15), as if regal in some way. They are "void of pride" and only "seem . . . to aspire" (like the Tower of Babel) toward the heavens (lines 3, 16). But, it is important to note, the poet has subtly introduced the association of trees and pride in the poem. The poet will eventually reveal that the trees are emblems for the sort of pride humanity once had, a pride of place in the vertical chain-of-being once enjoyed by Adam and Eve. It is an appropriate prelapsarian pride of place still enjoyed by nature, as represented by the trees, which remind mankind, once "more noble than those creatures all" (line 128), of its sin of pride that cost humanity its own pride of place in creation.

That there is trouble for the poet in her encounter with the Book of Nature is suggested in two places in the first unit of the poem. The initial instance remarks how the Sun's light "was shaded by the leavie tree" (line 24). Her vision of the "universe's eye" (line 27) is obstructed by the trees, a situation suggesting that even if nature is a wondrous work of art calling attention to the Logos as artist, it nonetheless interferes with the human ability to see the sun/son of God (a conventional seventeenth-century religious pun). This problem is reinforced by the poet's sense of being "Silent alone" in the "pathless paths" of the forest. Wandering within the Book of Nature, every feature of which is in effect a logogic site for humanity to hesitate over, provides no consolation for the poet searching for direction toward the Son, the sunlike Christ.

The theology behind this sense of the inadequacy of the Book of Nature for humanity is not difficult. In Eden, as we noted in chapter 1, Adam had two kinds of knowledge: *sapientia* and *scientia*. *Sapientia* was a special kind of intuitive wisdom by means of which Adam knew the names (the essential meaning) of natural things. *Scientia* was the kind of knowledge which came through the senses; it was a lower order of knowing to be guided by *sapientia*. After the Fall, Adam lost *sapientia*, and all of humanity after him became bereft of this capacity for intuitive wisdom. Adam's descendants have only *scientia*, but this dependence upon the senses for knowledge, through nature, is inadequate for discerning truth or for attaining salvation. The senses can deceive, and in the hierarchical scheme of things they were designed to obey reason—reason and will, in Puritan doctrine, comprise the soul—not serve as reason's sole source of information.

The poet in "Contemplations" has been reading the illuminated manuscript that is the Book of Nature, and she feels both obstructed from seeing the sun/Son directly and lost, as it were, in the pathless forest of logogic sites. She feels lost because, in contrast to Adam, she cannot *adequately* read the art of the Logos in nature. To be sure, the art of nature makes her think of God, even as *scientia* potentially teaches everyone certain basic truths, such as the difference between good and evil. But for postlapsarian humanity nature is not enough and in fact tends finally to indict humanity rather than to console it.[21]

Nature indicts humanity because it still evidences its vertical relation to the Creator, whereas humanity is *fallen* away from this vertical identity. This is the real reason why the poet feels isolated. She thinks she is so cut off from the vertical chain-of-being that even lowly insects produce a "little art" (line 61) far superior to her own verse. Confronted with this indictment, the poet finds herself trying to imitate the vertical trees by lifting her voice and "eyes to lofty skies" (line 53), only finally to find herself bereft of *sapiential* access to pure denotative referentiality. Bound to the temporal circumstance of postlapsarian logogic cruxes, to the threat of a Bablic verbal self-idolatry replete with dispersed obscure connotative corruptions of denotative meaning, the poet stands "mute" (line 64).

The Second Movement. As Edward Taylor writes, the soul was put in the wicker cage of the body to hymn divine praise ("Meditation 1.8"), and Anne Bradstreet likewise indicates, "To sing some song, my mazéd Muse thought meet. / My great Creator I would magnify" (lines 54-55). So the poet of "Contemplations" must overcome her muteness, must find her voice if she is to fulfill her obligation to write her verse in praise of God. To reanimate her voice she must turn away from the indictment of the Book of Nature. She must turn to the Book of Scripture, the Book given to humanity to inform reason through faith, as a partial replacement for lost *sapientia*. The poet has no hope of finding consolation in nature until she is guided through its logogic signs by the Bible.

Collective human memory, as recorded in the Bible, is the

subject of the second unit of "Contemplations" (stanzas 10 to 20).[22] This section of the poem rehearses the events in Eden and subsequent occurrences, including the metonymic story of Cain and Abel. This memory provides the poet with the explanation why she could not find provenance or empowerment for her own artistry in the Book of Nature. The reason is, simply, that Adam fell into a state of unstable meanings and lost a sense of humanity's initial denotative (vertical) relationship to the deity.

The poet cleverly echoes her association of this verticality and the trees in the first unit of the poem by noting in the second unit how Adam "Fancie[d] the apple, dangl[ing] on the tree" (line 74). Here again the image of the tree and the sin of pride are associated, an identification suggested not only in the first section but also made clearer in a later section of the poem. In this second unit, however, the poet indicates that the trees can be proud, in a restricted sense, because they remain "insensible of time" (line 123). This means that since they have not fallen into time, in some essential sense, the trees still enjoy eternity. Since they maintain their vertical relation to their creator, they can rightfully evince a proper sort of pride of place in the divine scheme of creation.

Humanity was once superior to the trees in its place in the vertical chain-of-being. Humanity was "by birth more noble than those creatures all" (line 128), more noble than the richly clad, stately trees. Like the trees, mankind "was made for endless immortality" (line 141). But humanity fell into "grief and care" (line 130), fell out of eternity and into time, fell (like the builders of the Tower of Babel) from denotative definition and into unstable connotative meanings. And the poet falls, again, into a momentary silence as she completes her review of biblical history.

The Third Movement. Now that the poet has recalled, as it were *reread*, the history recorded in the first part of the Book of Scripture, she can return to the Book of Nature. With her voice authorized and energized by the memory supplied by the Bible, she can seek out a better symbol than the trees to represent her fallen condition. In the third unit of the poem (stanzas 21 to 28) she replaces the symbol of the vertical trees with the emblem of the horizontal river.

In order to cue the reader that she has returned to the Book of Nature, the poet first opens the third unit with an echo of the first unit. Whereas she spoke earlier of "a stately oak," she opens the new section with a reference to "a stately elm" (line 142). But she quickly notes: "I once that loved the shady woods so well, / Now thought the rivers did the trees excel" (lines 146-147). The river, a conventional image for time or history,[23] provides the poet with a more congenial approach to the Book of Nature, with an emblem from which she can derive hope for her own salvation.

Whereas the trees, insensitive to time and evincing pride of place, indict humanity by reminding it of its loss of a vertical relationship to the deity, the river represents the horizontal temporal world, "A lonely place" in contrast to heaven (like Eden), a "beloved place" (lines 145, 154). However, even if the temporal world (symbolized by the river) is a place of isolation, it is nonetheless a realm "with pleasures dignified" (line 145) because, like all of nature, it still reflects the divine logogic artist. In other words, the temporal realm of unstable connotations evinces from within a divine definitive design concealed from most of fallen humanity.

The river possesses two characteristics that give the poet hope. First, the river overwhelms "rocks" (line 144) and any other seeming obstructions. In fact, the poet suggests that any apparent obstructions actually increase the flow of history in the way that rocks can form rapids in a stream and increase the force of the "stealing stream" (line 149): "I marked, nor crooks, nor rubs, that there did lie / Could hinder ought, but still augment its force" (lines 151-152). Second, the result of the poet's meditation on the flow of time, or history, contrasts with the result of her contemplation of the eternal as symbolized by the trees. The trees obstruct the poet's search for consolation, through a glimpse of the heavens or of the deity, because the symbolic verticality of the trees indicts rather than comforts humanity; in contrast the rivers, as a more accessible natural logogic sign for the poet, provide solace because their symbolic horizontalness is detectably resolved in "the longed-for ocean" (line 150). Just as the stream was a conventional symbol for history or time, the ocean was a conventional seventeenth-century emblem for eternity or the deity (for example, in Michael Wigglesworth's "A Short Discourse on Eternity," line 5). The emblem of the river, therefore, gives the poet hope when she interprets it and the Book of Nature through the memory of history as recorded in the Book of Scripture.

Now the poet expands her symbolic imagery to develop her theme about the nature of time. She develops an association between trees (the vertical, eternal) and birds, and between rivers (the horizontal, temporal) and fish.

The fish, conventionally symbolizing Christians, live in the stream of time. Some frisk wantonly and become prey (lines 170, 175). Moreover, they seem to wander somewhat aimlessly in their "liquid region" of time and leave "numerous fry" behind them, even as Adam did and his descendants still do, without knowing why (lines 163-168). Like postlapsarian humanity, the fish "know not . . . felicity" (line 169).

Birds, in contrast, represent the prelapsarian state. "Perched o'er [the poet's] head" (line 179), they are appropriately associated with the verticality of the trees. Like the trees in the poem, the birds are insensitive to time; a bird, the poet writes, remembers or "Reminds not what is past, nor what's to come dost fear" (line 190). The bird symbolizes humanity in its infancy, in its "summer season" (line 195) in Eden, where there were "no sad thoughts" (line 186), no memories, because there was no history, no time.

The Fourth Movement. After the break at the end of the third section of "Contemplations," Anne Bradstreet concludes her poem with a small final unit (stanzas 29 to 33) which emphasizes the nature of the temporality (history) into which humanity has fallen. In contrast to the bird's Edenic existence, life for humanity in the postlapsarian world is (as in the stream) an encounter with rocks, rubs, crooks—in short, an experience "wracked with pain" (line 207), with suffering and sad thoughts. For a while, the soul (imaged as a mariner in the fourth unit of the poem) can delude itself and "Sing . . . merrily" (line 213) as if it were (like a bird) in a prelapsarian state; for a while, especially in youth, it can be a "Fond fool" and try (like the poet in her own youth before she renounced the trees for the rivers) to identify with the verticality of the trees by thinking "this earth" is "heav'n's bower" (line 222). But the actualities of the stormy (line 216) temporal world, characterized by occluded meanings, will eventually destroy this illusion.

In the last stanza of "Contemplations" Anne Bradstreet summarizes her theme about "Time the fatal wrack of mortal things" (line 226). Time destroys all feeble efforts to erect vertical structures, pridefully erected structures (like the Tower of Babel) futilely implying a human immortality equivalent to the eternity represented by trees. Whereas the trees maintain their stateliness, their regality, "kings" fall into "oblivion" (line 227), even as their vertical, prideful "monuments" erode and are forgotten (lines 228-230). That mankind cannot imitate the trees is also suggested in the poet's reference to the mariner (soul) "steer[ing] his bark" (line 213), the mortal body. The poet could have chosen *ship* or *boat*, rather than the word *bark*; nothing in the line calls for that word specifically except that the allusion to a tree made horizontal in the stream of time reinforces the poet's point about the impropriety of trying to identify with the verticality of trees as an emblem of comfort in the world.

Only those whose names are "graved in the white stone" (line 232) will arrive at true treelike immortality in eternity. Only those whose names are engraved not on the time-doomed monuments, like vertical tombstones, but on the eternal upright white stone of Christ (Revelation 2.17), will regain their prelapsarian state. Only these elect saints will undergo the transformation of their horizontalness in the grave (their temporality, their morality) into a regained verticality in heaven (their eternity).

The Structural Emblem. In "Contemplations" Bradstreet's contrast of prelapsarian verticality with postlapsarian horizontalness forms an emblem that represents her theme about the nature of time and that accounts for the peculiar fragmented structure of her poem. That she has emblems in mind is most evident when she says of the river, "Thou emblem true of what I count the best" (line 160). Religious emblems were a commonplace in seventeenth-century religious poetry, and in "Contemplations" this emblem is the cross of Christ, the one locus of ultimate definition on which a biblically tutored Puritan contemplator of temporal logogic cruxes could indeed rely.

In "Contemplations" the poet alludes at least four times to the cross. Significantly, all of these allusions occur only in the last seven stanzas of the poem, as if to aid the reader in seeing the overall configuration of the imagery in the preceding stanzas. These four instances are specific logogic sites, where temporal connotation and eternal denotation twist together, in a poem that as a whole is an emblematic logogic crux where postlapsarian language conceals the humble poet's art and at the same time intimates a concealed divinely denotative design. When Bradstreet says that birds (emblems of prelapsarian humanity) know no "cruciating cares" (line 186), the truncated form of the word *excruciating* calls attention to its Latin rootword *crux* (cross). Similarly, the poet specifically refers to human "losses, *crosses*, and vexation" (line 209; emphasis added). And, finally, when she speaks of humanity as "wracked with pain" and of "Time" as "the fatal wrack of mortal things" (lines 207, 226), the word *wrack* not only means destroyer but also an instrument on which something can be stretched as if on a cross. By means of the word *wrack* the poet certainly indicates that time is the sure destroyer of a human life (for to be in time is to be fallen, "wracked with pain"); but her use of the word also suggests that the *wrack* of time potentially provides the opportunity for salvation, because time is, for the elect, a crucifixion transformed by the regenerative "fall" of Christ on the New Testament cross.

Underlying the theme of her poem, then, is the emblem of the Christian cross. Specifically, that cross is made up of two antithetical components: one, the human *memory* of the vertical eternal relationship (the trees, the birds) that mankind once had with God and that nature still evinces; the other, the human *experience* of the horizontal temporal (mortal) relationship (the river, the fish) that mankind now has with God. Every Christian, Bradstreet's poem suggests, must bear this cross comprised of memory (the vertical column of the cross) and experience (the horizontal beam of the cross). On this cross of memory and experience every Christian is "wracked," including Bradstreet negotiating the logogic sites of her postlapsarian reading of the Book of Nature as well as of her own verbal artistry. Contemplating the logogic crux of the emblem of the cross and pondering over the excruciating thoughts of her poem, Bradstreet wonders whether she is "wracked" in the sense that she will be spiritually destroyed (damned) or whether she is "wracked" in the sense that she will be stretched out, or burdened, in preparation for a restored eternal vertical resurrection (like Christ's) from the temporal, mortal horizontalness in the grave. The fact that her poem has precisely thirty-three stanzas, the same number as the age of Jesus when he died on the cross, encourages her hope.

Just as the emblem of the cross unites the opposition of verticality and horizontalness in the imagery of "Contemplations," it also informs the peculiar fragmented structure of the poem. The fissures, the gaps, the lacunae between the units of the poem make, at the structural level, the same point that is argued at the thematic and symbolic level of the poem. Anne Bradstreet knows that art has always been called a monument; and if the monuments of kings (lines 227-228) represent doomed, prideful, Babel-like attempts to derive comfort from a futile imitation of the eternal verticality of nature (trees), so too do the lines of poetry, arranged as they are in a vertical column. By fragmenting her poem into four movements Bradstreet distorts the vertical linearity of her poem. She refuses to let it give the impression of a neat vertical symmetry that would ironically serve as a tombstone memorializing her prideful attainment or as a Bablic monument to her ability as a poet. Like the Pilgrims, who according to Morton destroyed the monument of the maypole because they thought it was an

"Idoll," Bradstreet assails the perpendicular structure of her verse lest it serve as a representation of idolatrous poetic revelry. This destruction of vertical symmetry in "Contemplations" not only conforms to Bradstreet's lifelong desire to attain a proper sort of humility,[24] but also specifically suits her theme in the poem, the theme about the nature of time: the Christian's and the Christian artist's need to carry his or her cross. That cross is comprised of the recognition of the inaccessibility of a denotative vertical relationship with God (memory of the eternal) in the fallen world as well as of the related recognition of the potentially hopeful features of a horizontal connotative relationship with God (experience of the temporal, especially at the logogic site of human language).

The fragmentation of the vertical symmetry, or the linear development, of "Contemplations" is reinforced by the swelling out, as it were, of certain parts of Anne Bradstreet's poem. In the third unit, for example, the sudden introduction of another set of correlations—the fish and the birds—does not narratively advance the poem in a strictly linear way. On the contrary, that part of the third section of the poem is a sideways expansion, even as the river in the poem swells from a mere "stealing stream" to a wave-tossed body of water with ships and ports. The introduction of the bird and fish as symbols is more of a lateral swelling out, a horizontal embellishment, than an advancement of the linear movement of the poem. This feature appropriately augments the poet's theme and her underlying emblem: the need to remember that the verticality of prelapsarian existence is lost and must be transversed by the acceptance of the potentially hope-giving horizontalness of postlapsarian existence. Memory of that verticality in conjunction with the experience of this horizontalness is the cross each Christian must bear. This fact is the essential cross underlying what she describes in "On My Dear Grand Child Simon Bradstreet" as our temporal encounter with "bitter crosses" (line 14) in life.

Such a reading makes a case for the artistry of "Contemplations," a case that needs to be asserted far more than it has been to date. And such a reading provides one way of approaching Anne Bradstreet as an artist, a specifically Puritan artist who contemplates the logogic signs of nature and the logogic sites of human language, where the temporal and the eternal mysteriously intersect. If the poet cannot read this junction clearly concerning her own spiritual fate, she nonetheless finds hope there. And this hope is reinforced by her humble effort, like Richard Mather's, to fashion an art that conceals art: to disguise her own artfulness by revealing within it the hidden definitive (emblematic) artistry of the Logos.

Unfolding the Twisting Serpent
Edward Taylor's "Meditation 1.19"

In similarly *reading* Edward Taylor's "Meditation 1.19" as a text of partially recoverable authorial intention, we will first consider the coherent, even circular theological pattern of the poem as its focus shifts from creation (Adam, Genesis), to renewal of creation (Christ as Second Adam, New Testament), and to re-creation (the elect at the Second Coming, Revelation). Then, in terms of this theological pattern, we will discover the interrelation of the pagan and classical allusions in the poem. Subsequently, we will disclose how the meditation is coherently emblematic. We will remark not only the tradition behind the emblem of the serpent in the poem, but also specifically Taylor's artistic transformation of that single emblem into a new, but completely consistent guise in each stanza. Finally, we will relate this emblem, the pagan and biblical allusions, and the cyclic theological pattern to another metaphoric pattern in the meditation: the balancing of accounts, a specific logogic crux ideally defined by the hope-engendering perfect circle suggested by all the artistic elements in the poem.

Theological Pattern. "Meditation 1.19" presents Taylor's perception of the three most important moments in the history of the human race: the creation of the world (Edenic order), the Incarnation (the redeeming of creation), and the Last Judgment (the restoration of creation). This sequence suggests a wonderful denotative circle of perfection in which even fallen time, with its Bablic confusion of meanings, is contained within the divine order,[25] an archlike continuum linking paradise lost and paradise regained. This circular sequence (genesis, incarnation, second coming) orders the imagery of the meditation and is principally embodied in the central integrative emblem of the poem.

One strand of this imagery includes references to light lost and restored. The poem emphasizes the prevalence of darkness in the fallen world as a result of heaven being "knockt" by Hell (line 6).[26] The order of heaven seems, as Taylor's use of the word *knock* suggests, to have been struck down with a consequent apparent destabilization of its divine timing. In the postlapsarian world "The Worlds bright Eye's dash't out" (line 2). This image (bearing multiple implications, as we shall see) situates the poet in literal darkness, which later is identified as the time just prior to dawn. This absence of the sun readily reminds the poet of the spiritual murk in which he also finds himself, a darkness resulting from the fact that "The Candle of the World," Adam and the Second Adam even more than the sun, have been "blown out" (line 5) in the sense that they have left the earth long ago. And it reminds him, in another sense, of how the candleflame, the bright eye (pupil, or "Ball of Fire," line 14) of his once Adamic reason, has also been extinguished. The poet perceives a correspondence between the physical absence of Christ in the dark temporal world and the spiritual absence of an enlightened divine image in the "Bemidnighted" poet (line 3).

In the meditation this lack of light, in a double sense, is associated with the blackness of the grave, as if through its postlapsarian mortality humanity were, figuratively speaking, darkly entombed even while enjoying the apparent state of being alive in the material world. It is not only the sun or the Son who "lies buri'de in its grave" (line, 4), but somebody specific. For "Meditation 1.19" is an elegy. This elegy opens in the blackness of predawn morning with the poet standing before an open grave. The poet instructs his soul to take a good look at the ground and the hole dug into it (lines 1, 4).

This grave is for someone who, like the set sun and the absent Son, metaphorically is "The Candle of the World Blown out," "The World's bright Eye . . . dash't out." In the seventeenth century a human life was commonly imaged, in Francis Quarles's typical phrase, as a "blazing Tapour"; and the end of that life, again in Quarles's application of conventional imagery, as the vanishing of "That glorious *Sun*, what whilom shone so bright."[27] In Taylor's meditation the imagery of the extinguished candle and the set sun not only refers to Christ, Adam, and right reason, but also to someone who had died, someone important whose setting into the grave casts (in Taylor's opinion) the "World" of the Puritan community into darkness.

Pertinently, these two images commonly appear in Puritan elegies on deceased prominent people, especially ministers. Throughout the seventeenth century ministers were conventionally described as celestial bodies, especially stars,[28] imagery derived from Daniel 12:13. In his elegy on Thomas Shepard, as we shall see in chapter 3, Urian Oakes typically speaks of the deceased minister as a sun, a falling star, whose "glorious, shining Light's put out."[29] Who is the specific subject of Taylor's elegiac meditation, dated 14 November 1686, remains unknown, but it might be a neighboring minister not prominent in our contemporary recollection.[30] In the poem, however, the occasion of the burial of this person leads the poet to discover correspondences between this deceased person, the set sun, the fallen Adam, the departed Second Adam, and the blinded eye of reason as reminders of human mortality, which can result in the spiritual death of any reasonless— "befoold" (line 19)—soul condemned to the eternal gravelike darkness of hell.

Throughout the poem death, the grave, and hell are correlated. In the second stanza the poet notes how the grave site has filled with water, not surprising given the nature of November weather in New England. Looking at this water-filled grave, the poet remarks that "this World [is] all filld up to the brim / With Sins, Deaths, Divills, Crowding men to Hell" (lines 7-8). He also speaks in the third stanza of "the Setting Sun" as a falling star that has "Dropt like a Ball of Fire into the Seas" (lines 13-14). His coalescence of darkness, mortality, and water imagistically recalls the story of creation in Genesis and the predictions of Revelation.

In Genesis (Geneva version) creation occurs when "the earth was without forme & voyde and darknes was upon the depe, & the Spirit of God moved upon the waters" (1:2). In traditional typological terms this image of the ocean, the sea, the deep in Genesis represents chaos, the void out of which the deity created a beautiful order and the vacuity into which Satan lures fallen humanity. The same image, the deep as chaos, informs Revelation, especially in reference to "the great dragon, that old serpent, called the devil and Satan" (12.9). The image of "the flood, which the dragon had cast out of his mouth" (Revelation 12:16) is patristically identified with the void of nonbeing, preceding creation in Genesis. This image of the flood, the primal deep spewed forth by leviathan, readily coalesces with the related imagery of nonbeing (darkness, the grave, death) in Taylor's poem.

In this meditation these three images (darkness, the grave, and water) are related to Satan, who is particularly evident in the reference to "the Serpents Head" (line 29). This traditional Christian correspondence of the devil with the serpent principally derives from the account of the fall in Genesis, in which the snake serves as Lucifer's agent, and from the account of the last battle in Relevation, in which the great dragon is (as we saw) called Satan and specifically associated with the serpent in Eden. In Renaissance lore, a serpent becomes a dragon by eating one of its own kind,[31] and the dragon (in, for example, stories about St. George) typically symbolizes the bringer of death. The humans it consumes enter the deeps of its stomach; death was imaged in these Renaissance stories as a fatal submergence underwater in the belly of the dragon. These stories are based on exegetical readings of leviathan as the dark postlapsarian world, and of the fatal existence of Adam's mortal progeny in the belly of this beast.[32] The threat of death in the watery stomach of the demonic dragon represents the effort of Satan to undo creation, to return it to the void, nonbeing of the pre-creation deep. This correspondence in Renaissance lore between the great dragon (serpent, devil), death (the grave), darkness, and the deep lies behind Taylor's ready merging of these images in "Meditation 1.19."

In this poem the combined imagery of darkness, the grave, water, and the serpent are brought full circle. The poet, echoing the Wise Men who proclaimed their sight of the "starre in the East" (Matt. 2.2; cf. Revelation 6:8), instructs himself "to the East come, run: / You'l meet the morn Shrinde with its flouring Rayes" (lines 15-16). The morning sun is about to rise and revive the hope of the languishing "Wan" soul (line 1), so bereft of life-renewing illumination; sunrise symbolizes the promise of the risen Son concerning the resurrection of the elect sons of God on the last day. The return of the sun adumbrates the reappearance of the Son at the Second Coming, when the Second Adam will restore the elect (possibly including the poet and the deceased subject of his elegy) to their sunny golden Adamic state.

The "flouring Rayes" of this returned sun/Son suggest the illuminating actual presence of Christ in the material realm again, the rekindling of the candleflame of the bright eye of reason (*sapientia* and *scientia*) in the elect, and the revivification of Adamic life, physically and spiritually, in the saints. The meanings of "Flouring" in Taylor's time include "flourishing"; and the return of light, in the multiple ways his imagery suggests, conveys a sense of how the resurrected elect will certainly flourish. Indeed, the chosen will no longer look "Wan" or "palde" (lines 1, 3), but now enlightened by the golden light of the returned Son, the elect will be restored to their golden (tanned) Edenic state (cf. Taylor's "Meditation 1.8," line 10).

"Flouring" in Taylor's time also meant "flowering," and as Taylor's personal experience with agriculture taught him, the plants he knew did not flower without sunlight. In a prolonged darkness flowers, such as eyebright, would wither until they were "blown" (line 5). Similarly, there is no flowering of the affections of the soul without the rekindling of the "bright Eye" of reason by the light of the risen Christ surrounded by rays of light which seem like flower petals ("flouring Rayes"). This reference to flowering in Taylor's meditation not only accords with his imagery of light but also with his emphasis on the grave. Just as the Second Coming ends darkness, it also ends death. The return of the Son converts the grave-waste of fallen humanity—"thou art dust, and to dust shalt thou returne" (Genesis 3:19)—into reformed life, renewed ground, even as the sun transforms the "Dunghill" (line 12) into a garden.[33] As new life emerges from death in nature, each saint, like "The Sun of Righteousness," will rise "out of's Grave" (line 34).

The return of the sun will dry up the excess of November rain and leave useful, orderly "brooke[s]" (line 18). This effect of the sun is necessary if flowers are to flourish, and the Second Coming of the Son (reasserting the role of the Logos in Genesis) will likewise push back the dark chaos of the Serpent's death-dealing deep so that the seemingly "blown" saints may revive. In "Meditation 1.19" Taylor characteristically suggests that the Incarnation is a reaffirmation of creation and that the Second Coming will be a restoration of the order of Eden, a paradise regained. His poem emphasizes the prophecy in Genesis ("He shal breake thine head" [3:15]) and of Revelation ("there was no more sea" and "no night" [21:1, 25]). This eventual mastery over the great dragon and over the dark watery chaos of its interior is alluded to in the poem when Christ is imaged as a mauler of the serpent's head (line 29).

In this way the four main patterns of imagery and the theological thought underlying them in "Meditation 1.19" form a coherent circle of meaning. Relying on Genesis and Revelation, Taylor stresses the transformation of darkness (void) into light, of the grave (death) into new flowering and flourishing life, of the deep (chaos) into restored order, and of the serpent's rampage (evil) into complete submission. In this way the poet imitates the denotative balanced account (line 24) provided by the first and the last books of scripture, which prophesy how God will circuitously settle accounts and rebalance the order of His creation.

The Pagan and the Biblical. Taylor's own balanced account in his poem includes managing pagan lore beyond the mere notion that a serpent becomes a dragon by eating one of its own kind. The pagans of antiquity, Puritans like Taylor believed, had read the Book of Nature by the limited light of their corrupted reason, specifically by means of *scientia;* and these pagans, Puritans also believed, had heard Old Testament stories in distorted versions. As a result, Puritan divines thought that in some fundamental sense pagan myths and legends reflect truth in disguised form.[34] So, Puritan ministers maintained, when pagan stories were explicated in biblical terms, the resultant readings were not inventions but discourses of disguised versions of Old Testament types adumbrating the New Testament antitype. Of the classical allusions in "Meditation 1.19" the most prominent refer to the labors of Hercules.

That Hercules figures in this poem is perhaps most evident in the last stanza, which indicates that "The Sun of Righteousness" (sun/Son) is "a Gyant" who "awoke" and "rose out of's Grave" (lines 33-34). The stanza indicates as well that the elect, related to Christ through the Incarnation, share in this condition of giantism. This condition fascinates Taylor, who twenty years later in a incomplete long poem on excavated mammoth bones specifically referred to the encounter between the giant Antaeus and "his Superiour," Hercules (lines 89-98).[35] In Taylor's mind, perverted giantism is associated with the Satanic leviathan, divine giantism with the sunlike Son, who as the Second Adam restores the saints to their Adamic status as the spiritual giants of the earth.

According to classical legends, terrible earthborn giants with snaky long hair and beards, as well as serpent tails for feet, plotted a rebellious assault against Zeus. They could be killed only by a lion-skinned mortal, Hercules. The giants Hercules encountered in his eleventh labor were born from Mother Earth, and so every time they were knocked to the ground in combat they quickly sprung up newly revived because this was their native ground.[36] Typically Antaeus, a huge giant of Libya who was the son of Poseidon and Ge (mother earth), grew stronger every time he touched the earth. Hercules destroyed him and the other rebellious sons of the gods by removing them from their native ground.

Taylor detects a correspondence between this classical account and the biblical story about the sons of God in Genesis (6:2-4): "the sonnes of God sawe the daughters of men that they were faire, and they take them wives of all that they liked"; "there were gyants in the earth in those dayes: yea, and after that the sonnes of God came unto the daughters of men, and they had borne them children, these were mightie men." In some traditions these sons of God are identified as angels who rebelled against their mission to teach humanity truth and justice, and who mated with earthly women and begot evil giants.[37] The descendants of these giants ("the sons of God") are slain by Christ, the Son of God, who in Renaissance Christian imagery is often allied with Hercules. Like Hercules, Christ separates the damned from the ground of their behavior by revealing, as the opening line of "Meditation 1.19" suggests, that the ground (earth, dust) of their actions is only the grave (death).

As the poem opens, the poet stares at an excavated grave site and admonishes, "Looke till thy Looks look Wan, my Soule; here's ground" (line 1). Here is mere earth, the dust to which all postlapsarian humanity must return. This literal fact also allegorically warns of the eternal spiritual death that awaits the soul that relies on that dusty soil as its only ground (fundamental constituent) of being. But Hercules-like Christ redeems this earthly ground by removing the evil ("Pious Fraud") that has "Curst" it (lines 10, 13; cf. line 27) and its blown plants (elect), and thereby He reveals the more fundamental, spiritual ground of human existence: "ye, being rooted and grounded in love" (Ephesians 3:17). On this reclaimed ground of divine love humanity's Adamic giant stature can once again flourish (bloom), especially in the light of the restored bright eye of reason. Appropriately, at the end of "Meditation 1.19" Christ and the restored elect are imaged as genuine Herculean figures gladiatorially mauling the head of gigantic leviathan.

This last image is important; for in Taylor's poem Hercules is associated not only with Christ, the Son of God who defeats the descendants of the rebellious sons (angels) of God, reclaims humanity's native ground of being, and recovers humanity's rightful place as gigantic sons-of-God. In the meditation Hercules is also associated with the Christ who harrows hell and defeats the great dragon. Hercules performs his most difficult task (his twelfth labor) when he descends into Hades, sets Theseus free, and outwits the prince of that infernal place. In Taylor's poem, the resurrected Christly giant similarly "brake[s] down" the "Bars and Gates of Hell" with His penetrating flourishing rays, and having harrowed hell He emerges "out of's Grave" (lines 30, 34), out of the pit of hell's mouth.

Moreover, in some versions of his eleventh labor, Hercules slays the serpent Ladon, who guards the tree of golden apples in the garden of the Hesperides. This myth apparently suggests to Taylor the biblical prophecy of Christ's slaying the great dragon, who is identified in Revelation as Satan and who is depicted in Genesis as the barrier between the tree of life and once-golden humanity. Possibly this allusion to the serpent Ladon and the tree of golden apples also corresponds for Taylor to the role of Hercules as the slayer of man-eating birds in his fifth labor and the killer of sea-monsters in his second and sixth labors, for the life-destroying great dragon of Revelation is winged and casts the deep of chaos from its mouth.[38] And, finally, this allusion recalls the details that the evil giants slain by Hercules/Christ had snaky hair and beards as well as serpent-tails for legs. Fittingly, Taylor's poem concludes with an image of the Herculean Christ rising out of "the Seas" of chaos (into which He fell through the Incarnation), silencing the self-applauding "Clap" of the dragonlike "Wings" of devils, and mauling the gigantic "Serpent Head" of leviathan (lines 14, 12, 29).

The classical versions of Hercules's destruction of the evil giant progeny of the rebellious sons of gods, his harrowing of Hades, and his defeat of the serpent guarding the tree of golden apples in the gardens of the Hesperides suggest to Taylor the antitypical New Testament activities of Christ. And these Classical stories, as a result, readily reinforce Taylor's artistic integration of his images of the serpent (great dragon, devil), the grave (death), darkness, and the deep (sin) in "Meditation 1.19," especially in terms of the circular theological pattern biblically established in Genesis and Revelation. The sway of the rebellious sons of God in Genesis will be supplanted by the triumph of the Herculean Son of God and of the restored Adamic sons of God (Revelation 2:18, 21:7). Then the separation of humanity in Genesis from its true native ground (Edenic immorality) will end with the casting of the dragon/serpent deep "into the earth," into hell, by the Herculean Christ (Relevation 12:9) and with the return of the saints to a "new heaven, and a new earth" (Revelation 21:1). And then the curse of death (mortality) imposed on humanity in Genesis will be dispelled for the elect by the Herculean Christ, who will harrow hell (imaged as the grave, void, and deep) so that "the sea gave up her dead, which were in her, and death and hell delivered up the dead, which were in them" (Revelation 20:13).

Moreover, this circular pattern in the poem, from the deprivations recorded in Genesis to the restorations prophesied in Revelation, includes the fact that Hercules wore a lion skin. Hercules slew the seemingly invulnerable lion of Nemea in its hell-like cavern and clothed himself in its skin. This episode corresponds, in Taylor's Christian mind, to the story of David's defeat of a lion (I Samuel 17:34-37), for Hercules is for Taylor a Classical version of the Davidic type adumbrating Christ. In "Meditation 1.19" Taylor specifically refers to how "Gods mikewhite Lamb" lays "these Lyons dead" (lines 9, 17). The demonic beast that howls like a lion (Relevation 4:7) will be overcome by the lamb (Relevation 12:11). Beneath the lion skin is the Herculean Christ, but Christ is also the sacrificial lamb of Revelation (5:6, 12): "stode a Lambe as thogh he had bene killed"; "the Lambe that was killed to receive power, and riches, and wisdome, and strength, & honour, and glorie, and praise." The Lamb of God falls to the ground and revives again, as a celestial creature surpassing "nede of the sunne" (Revelation 21:23) and as the proper gigantic Son of God restored to His native ground.

In short, the demonic lion is slain by the divine lamb, which had at first appeared to have been slain by this lion (line 10); and unlike the lion, the lamb revives again and dons the lion's skin. In Taylor's poem these images specifically refer to God's angry justice (lion) and God's tender mercy (lamb). In *Gods Determinations*, as we saw in chapter 1, Taylor similarly dramatizes how the forces of divine justice (law, the covenant of works) and divine mercy (gospel, the covenant of grace) dynamically contest with each other in the fallen temporal world. Mercy (Lamb, Christ, Hercules) is, as it were, first consumed (the crucifixion, death) by Justice (God's wrath), imaged in Revelation (9:8) and in "Meditation 1.19" (line 10) as plaguey demonic forces which, like "the teeth of lions," mortally "worry" (tear and greedily swallow) humanity; but these forces have cause to "worry" because the sacrificial lamb emerges victorious (the resurrection, immortality) as if concealed under the skin of divine Justice. In this way, "with Justices Acquittance in his hand," he "Dasht out all Curses from the Covenant [of Works]" (lines 27-28) and undoes the dashing out of the "Worlds Bright Eye" (Christ, the image of God in Adamic reason, the human Edenic heritage as a giant son of God). In this way, theologically and aesthetically, Taylor keeps a balanced account in his poem, which traces the circuitous linkage between the history of Genesis and the prophecies of Revelation.

The Emblem. In "Meditation 1.19," as we have observed so far, the images of the serpent (great dragon, devil), the grave (death), darkness (lost golden light), and the deep (voidlike sin), as well as the allusions to Hercules's defeat of the giant, his slaying of both the dragon/serpent and the lion, and his harrowing of Hades are all mutually, intricately interwoven in terms of several related themes in Genesis and Revelation. But underlying this interweaving, and augmenting its artistic tensile strength, is a still more fundamental bond: an emblem functioning as a specific logogic site where secular meanings and divine definitions especially coalesce in a meditation that as a whole is a logogic crux for the poet. This emblem informs each of Taylor's six stanzas and, like Bradstreet's emblem, reveals a divine artistic design concealed within the poet's artistry superficially characterized by a nearly chaotic proliferation of Bablic meanings.

One way of appreciating this emblem in "Meditation 1.19" is to consider for a moment a related device in "Meditation 1.8." In this earlier poem the recurrent figure of the arch informs each stanza. It initially appears as a night sky and horizon beneath which the poet stands on the ground; then as a cage in which the grounded birdlike soul longs to ascend beyond the confines of the body and the physical universe; then as an inverted barrel with the stars looking like sparse flour crumbs of the inaccessible bread of life; then as God's bowel filled with the Son being ground in gristmill fashion into the bread of life needed to fill the empty barrel of creation; then as the rising (resurrecting) of the dough of this divine bread of life; and finally as an inverted crystal (Christ-made) meal bowl so full of the risen bread of life that manna from heaven ends the famine by falling into the mouth of the crying saint/bird.[39] While its specific individualized macrocosmic and microcosmic meanings wondrously and terrifyingly proliferate for the poet, the single emblematic configuration of the arch remains constant throughout "Meditation 1.8"

"Meditation 1.19" interestingly inverts this very image of the arch, and in every stanza appears the emblematic figure of a pitlike cavity in the earth. The poem opens with the poet standing before an excavated grave site. This craterlike depression in the ground suggests to him that a falling star has crashed into the earth. The mention of "the sparkling sun" that "lies buri'de in its grave" (lines 3-4) refers to (1) the literal person (possibly a fellow minister) about to be interred, (2) the fall of Adam into mortality, (3) the death of Christ, and (4) the eschatological fall of the sun and the stars into the seas and the earth (Relevation 6:12, 8:10, 9:1). As we have noted, in Puritan culture ministers were routinely likened to celestial bodies, Adam (imprinted with the divine image) was considered the sunlike golden "Candle of the World" (line 5), and the Second Adam was thought to be the resuscitating sunlike Son of God. When each of these falls into darkness (death, the grave), it is as if the "Worlds bright Eye's dasht out" (line 2), as if the sun or a star has apocalyptically fallen into the earth. The crater made by the impact of the fall of Adam and the sacrificial death of the Second Adam is a grave, an inversion of the arch of heaven.

In the second stanza, the poet without adequate light looks wan—fearful, unhealthy, corpselike—as he stares at the memento mori of this dismal, sea-colored (wan) grave. He notices that it has "filld up to the brim" with sin (line 7), an image derived from the association of evil and water in Genesis and Revelation, most specifically (as we noted) in the reference to the spewing forth of chaos from the dragon's mouth. The poet's focus on a gravesite filled with water is appropriate given the fact that his poem was written during a rainy month in New England; but the literal occasion is less important than the symbolic significance of this figure in the poem.

The grave is filled with the "Sins, Deaths, Devills, Crowding men to Hell" (line 8). The gravesite, the crater in the earth seemingly made by a falling star, is the gateway to hell, which apparently in this poem is situated at the center of the earth. To the chaotic deep of this hell, fallen, mortal humanity has been led by sin. Here the cursed are consumed by scavenger devils, "Dunghill Cocks"[40] and black "Crow[s]" like the man-eating birds encountered by Hercules; these carrion eaters "Clap their Wings" (lines 11-12)—that is (as *clap* trebly suggests) applaud themselves, make a deal with Satan, and sentence their victims high-handedly—as they wait at the gateway of hell in a "Pious Fraud" of offering protection under their wings while actually crowding (pressing, herding) reprobates toward eternal oblivion. The scavenger nature of these creatures reminds the corpse-hued poet of the dreadful activity of decomposition (consumption) of the flesh that occurs in the grave.

This picture of the grave as a declivity in the earth filled up with rainwater, as the gateway to hell's decomposing deep, is modified in the third stanza to include the poet's vision of an apocalyptic fall of the sun itself into the watery grave of the bowl-like ocean. The blackness of the excavated gravesite is like the physical and spiritual darkness of the night, a kind of entombment in which postlapsarian humanity finds itself. It is "as if the Setting Sun: / Dropt like a Ball of Fire into the Seas" (lines 13-14).

Extending the connection between the deep and decomposing flesh, the fourth stanza transforms the inverted arch (represented so far by a fallen-star crater, a water-filled grave, a gateway hole to hell, and an ocean-filled pit) into a stomach digesting human remains. The man-eating creatures, "Rampant Fiends," in this stomachlike grave make "Gall" out of human remains (lines 19-20), even as the fallen star predicted in Revelation (8:10-11) makes bitter and poisonous the sea into which it falls. This end product of gall (secretions of the liver, poison, venom, and filth) signifies a failure to attain the higher ends of digestion, which according to Galenic physiology is thought.[41]

Moreover, the mindless scavengers of human carrion do not consume anything nutritive or vital. They cannibalize only the "Winding sheete" which "pale[d] round" (lines, 3, 20) Christ and the elect; that is to say, they consume only Christ's and the elect's flesh, the drippings (windings) on the side of their candlelike lives, not their spirit, not their candleflame. They consume only the shroudlike flesh, the dust from which humanity is formed and to which it must return.[42] Only "the light of the wicked shal be put out" (Proverbs 24:20), and the chosen soul smitten "downe to the earth" and "laied in the darkness" will not be left "in the grave" (Psalms 16:10, 143:3). In other words, the serpent devours filthy ground rather than the spiritual ground, the fundamental constituency, of the lives of the saints. As a result these choleric eaters of human carrion will be galled (bitterly exasperated) and ironically develop problems that proper amounts of gall normally cure.[43] Specifically they will develop "Heart-ach," disappointment and heartburn (the putrefactive fermentation of food in their stomach). And they will develop a painful swollen "Inflammation of the lungs" (lines 21, 22), as if the legendary fire breathed by these hellish dragons were like brimstone forced inward by their own brim-filling (line 7) chaotic waters and turned upon themselves by the undigestible rekindled candleflame of the saints resistantly burning in the deeps of their stomachs.

This stomach, the fifth stanza indicates, is inside the great dragon. In this stanza the crater, the gravesite, the gateway to hell, the pit of the deep, and the bowl-like declivity of the stomach become the dragon's mouth, hell's mouth on "the Serpents Head." And, in the sixth stanza, out of this serpentine mouth emerges Christ, the Herculean hero clad in the lion-skin of divine justice who harrows hell, restores the elect to their golden Edenic gigantic stature, poisons (galls) the evil giant progeny of the rebellious sons of God, and recreates order out of the deep by mauling the head of the serpent, the great dragon.

Behind Taylor's image of the grave as the serpent's mouth are several pagan and Christian pictorial representations prevalent during the Renaissance. The frontispiece of Francis Quarles's *Emblems* (1635) typically depicts the tree of life with humanity as a child who is completely vulnerable to a vicious-looking viper. The lower detail of that frontispiece, in which the demonic serpent symbolically ruptures the frame (form, order, creation) of the picture itself, suggests that the butterfly soul *(anima)* is bitten and devoured by the serpent's mouth *(malum)*, with the result of a mortal fall into time (imaged by the skull and hourglass) and into self-destructive folly (imaged by the jester and wilted blown flower of life). Human life is doomed to mortality (the mouth of the grave) because it has been consumed by the serpent.

This figure is more explicitly depicted in the scene of the Last Judgment on the south portal of the cathedral at Chartres. To the left of the judging Christ are the damned; some are carried and some are driven as they are crowded into the huge fiery mouth of leviathan, the great dragon that represents hell in Revelation.[44] This scene is remarkably similar to Taylor's image of "Divills, Crowding men to Hell" (line 8), and his equation of hell's gateway with the grave and with the serpent's mouth.

Also notable is the correspondence between Taylor's picture of the emergence of Christ and the elect from this demonic dragon's mouth to another emblem prevalent during the Renaissance. Although this emblem is very old, dating at least from the coins of Alexander the Great, an excellent version of it occurs as the first emblem of Andreae Alciati's *Emblemata*, a work that was so popular it was translated into many languages and saw numerous editions. The first emblem of the 1621 English edition of *Emblemata* shows the tree of life, inside of which is a giant serpent with a human figure half emerged from its mouth. Christians might have seen in this split-open tree (so the viewer can see the interior) and in this seemingly half-swallowed human the fate of fallen mankind, the blight on the tree of life wrought by the demonic serpent who (as Quarles's emblem and Taylor's imagery suggest) violates the order of creation and devours humanity. But in fact Alciati has reproduced a pagan image of a different order of meaning, as his Latin poem beneath the emblem notes. In this poem Alciati remarks the myth that the nobility of humanity originate from a race generated by the seed of Jove in the guise of a snake. So the birth of the nobility, the sons of Jove (God), is represented as an emergence from a serpent's mouth.

In pagan lore serpents are often more subtle than any of the other beasts of the field and so sometimes represent wisdom; in other stories, serpents, like the giant sons of God in both Classical and biblical accounts, rebel against carrying out their mission to humanity and also steal immortality from humanity.[45] That such alternative or parallel traditions to the Christian interpretation of the serpent were available to Taylor in early commentaries on the Old Testament is evident in his focus on the Mosaic serpent of brass in "Meditation 2.61."[46]

In "Meditation 1.19" Taylor plays off the alternative, pagan notion of the serpent typically represented in Alciati's emblem. If death is an entry into the gravelike mouth of leviathan (as imaged at Chartres), then the resurrection of the elect, similar to Christ after harrowing hell, would be equivalent to springing out of that mouth. In terms of Taylor's poem, this issuance of the chosen from the maw of the great dragon explains one sense in which the serpentine devils fail in the poem to flourish in their devouring of the saints; the elect do not proceed along the alimentary canal to the anus of the great dragon, to produce the "Dunghill" of which it is so fond. The saints, who drink at "the brooke" (line 18) of Christ's blood, are unbrookable (undigestible) for Satan, and must be spewed out of the deep of the belly of leviathan, thereby fulfilling the prediction that "the sea . . . and death and hell" will deliver "up the dead, which were in them" (Relevation 20:13). This emergence of the saints from the mouth of the great dragon will restore the elect to the noble dignity that the pagan emblem foreshadowingly represents. In this way, in terms of Taylor's Christian management of imagery in his meditation, the chosen sons of God regain the gigantic stature of Adam.

In this way, too, the perverted role of the serpent will be reversed; once again the serpent, the rebellious devourer of humanity, will fulfill its legendary mission as a life-giving servant and messenger of the deity. This transformation of the great dragon corresponds to the metamorphosis (through the death and resurrection of Christ) of the death-dealing lion of divine Justice (wrath) into the life-restoring lamb of divine mercy (love). Once again in the balanced account (design) concealed within his meditation Taylor has integrated pagan and Christian notions, and in the process has shown in what sense the wan light of the pagan belief is truly reflective of radiant Christian truth.

Balancing Accounts. An explicit reference to "Ballancing Accounts" (line 24) occurs in the fourth stanza of Taylor's meditation, where it serves as a specific logogic site apropos the recurrent emblem (itself a logogic crux) in the poem (as a whole a logogic crux). As the preceeding commentary has suggested, this idea that everything comes full circle, integrating the eternal and the temporal, informs Taylor's meditation at every point. This denotative divine reality lies concealed within, as Bradford observed, "the mutable things of this unstable world," within the very instability of temporal connotative meanings represented by the apparent disorder at the surface level of Taylor's meditation. This definitive cohesive design lies concealed (like the merciful lamb under the skin of the wrathful lion) within the temporal bifurcations highlighted by Satan in *Gods Determinations*. And this eternal configuration lies as a hidden potentiality, as a possible canceling of the saint's indebtedness, within the necessity of the eventual reckoning of that saint's indebtedness, for which he or she will certainly give an account at the Last Judgment. For the poet to meditate on the ramifications of the image of balanced accounts is to hesitate over a logogic site where hope in redeeming eternal definition and despair over damning temporal meanings intersect. To maintain hope, Taylor reveals the balancing divine art concealed within his unbalanced corrupt artfulness.

At the theological level, the reference to balanced accounts specifically alludes to the "Cancelling [of] the Bond," the "crossing out" (so to speak) of the agreement, indebtedness, obligation, or bondage resulting from the human default in the "Covenant" of Works (lines 23, 27). The resurrected Son emerges from "the Counthouse" (line 25), the place of divine account-keeping, the way the sun re-emerges from the counthouse of the zodiac.[47] These images suggest that the knock of time, disturbed by the knock by Satan, is reestablished (the clocklike order of creation reaffirmed) by the return of the Son (sun). The Son "Hath Justices Acquittance in his hand" (line 28), a release in writing (the Covenant of Grace) for the knocked down saints. Restored to cosmic harmony, the saints find their debt paid in full (line 23). Reset (like a clock) and also thus reckoned (released from an accountlike indebtedness), the elect are born again, their "Reckoning day" ending their spiritual pregnancy. They are restored to their noble, giant Adamic stature, returned to the true *ground* (divine love, immortality) of their heritage as the sons of God.

This theological sense of judicially balanced accounts in the poem draws as well upon the Renaissance appreciation of government and law as fundamental expressions of order,[48] and this restoration of cosmic order informs the circularity of the images in Taylor's meditation. The setting of the sun in the west, as if sunken into the inverted arch of the sea, is followed in the poem by the rising of the sun in the east toward the arch of the heavens, just as the death of the Son of God is followed by His resurrection and ascension. Likewise, the apparent downfall of the order of nature, seemingly submerged into the black void of the primal deep preceding creation, is reversed by its restoration at the Second Coming. Then the darkened world of mortality and time will be transformed into immortality and eternity within the Edenic golden light of "flouring Rayes" (line 16), even as new flowers are produced on the dungy soil (line 12) created by the death of previous flowers (life). Relatedly, the distortions of pagan myths, such as the labors of Hercules or the derivation of nobility from the serpent's mouth, are allied with and illuminated by biblical truth in a circular pattern in the poem. And, finally, human fatality within the dark interior of the great dragon is reversed by the vomiting out of the saints into renewed eternal golden life, where the fallen Adamic sons of God regain their noble stature as giants. In these ways the history of Genesis is encompassed within the prophecies of Revelation.

Everything will come full circle when the Second Coming cancels "the Bond" by "making Pay" (line 23) not only in the sense that the indictment against humanity will be discharged but also in the sense that the serpent's ropelike bounding or bondage of humanity in fallen time will be slackened, payed out. The sinuous twists of fallen time, the serpent's "Sting" (line 35) or rope that "fells" bound humanity, will be undone. As the lower detail of Quarles's frontispiece to *Emblems* indicates, the contortions of the serpent correspond to the circuit of time itself. When time ends, the bond of the serpent's bondage of humanity will be undone. Then the inverted arch of the serpent's mouth (the grave) will be joined to the arch of the heavens, reforming a perfect circle.

The reaffirmation, by the Second Coming, of this perfect circle is also imaged by Taylor as an unfolding, a *disclosure* that *uncoils* the bounds of the serpent. Similar to Bradford's conceit of the serpent's sly winding that untwists sacred bonds, Taylor's serpent seemingly determines the twists in the inverted arch of human history. As we saw in the meditation, in the great dragon's mouth (mortal life, the grave, hell's mouth) the devouring of the undigestible saints secures for the devil only their nonnutritive "Winding sheete" "palde round" (lines 20, 3) their flesh (dust, candle drippings). This representation (shroud) of the writhing of the serpent around humanity is all that the great dragon gets, and in this sense leviathan paradoxically sets the saints free by consuming the very bond (mortgage, mortality) he has on fallen humanity. As a result, he develops heartache not only because the rekindled candleflame of the saints burns in his stomach or because he is disappointed in his scheme, but also, and more significantly, because in consuming his bond on humanity he has unfolded (disclosed) God's hidden plan and unfolded (undone) his reason for being. In this way what lies between the heavenly arch and the hellish inverted arch is unscrolled, and the perfect circle, or bond, formed by these two arches is revealed.

And this unwinding of the mortality (shroud) of the saints represents the unscrolling of the sheet of Justice's acquittal in Christ's hand at the Last Judgment. When that sheet was scrolled, it (like human history) was coiled like the serpent. Unwound, this sheet presents balanced accounts by sentencing the damned (no better than dust) to the mouth of the great dragon and by saving the chosen from the eternal decomposition in the gravelike stomach of great dragon. The saints now find that their debt has been canceled, paid, and struck over ("crossed out") by the inscribing rays of the Son. Now the elect truly sing God's praise because they are joyful, with their bright (sunlike, candleflamelike) eye of reason restored, by which they can read the unscrolled sheet of the true narrative of history and of their lives. They will also sing joyfully because this unfolding disclosure of the narrative of history at the end of time "In Flashing Folds" (line 26), on golden sheets *(folds)* of paper, revealingly unfolds the serpent. In this sense the sheets on which the elect would pen their praise would be unscrolled, even as would be the sheet of their life and of human history (destiny).

Characteristically Taylor cannot presumptuously claim to be among these elect. Nevertheless, nervously hesitating over the logogic site of his meditation (especially its emblem of declivity and its relation to the image of balanced accounts), he readily fantasizes how it might feel to be able to sing God's praises were the serpent's bonds on his life to be uncoiled. He envisions himself in a healthier state than his present wan and fearful condition, and he fancies that then he would risk the placement of his own foot on the serpent's neck (line 35); in this way the poet cautiously inserts his imagined elect self in the corner of the typological picture in the poem,[49] in which Christ stands on the serpent's head so that the saint might be able to step safely on its neck. Safe from being unbalanced by the unwound serpent on which he stands, the poet imagines that he might now be able poetically to give a harmonious account of the wonderful denotative divine balancing of accounts.

Caught in the bounds of fallen time, however, his poem is connotatively sinuous indeed, replete with syntactic, imagistic, and thematic entanglements. The surface disorder of his meditation suggests how the serpent's bond exerts its entwining hold on the fallen poet and his poem, replete with doubletalk. Yet, this double-talk in the meditation is a logogic site where the threat of dispersed meaning (the demise of the poet) intersects with the promise of reclaimed referentiality (the redemption of the poet). Artistically concealed beneath the surface of the various kinds of convolutions evident in the proliferation of meanings are subtle coalescences and an ultimate circularity disclosing the unifying denotative artistry of God revealed in Genesis and Revelation.

These underlying features not only echo the prophecies of scripture but also hint to God that this particular singer (poet) perhaps possesses a certain latent ability that might be especially useful to the deity. By artistically managing an underlying, hidden coalescence of imagery in terms of an ultimate divine circularity and, as well, by integrating this imagery and pattern through a central denotative emblem, the poet seeks God's attention. Taylor's meditation intimates that he tries to unfold (disclose) the serpent's ultimate defeat at the end of the sinuous windings of history and, at the same time, that he tries to unravel his own song to God from the bond of Bablic twisted rhetoric, the shroudlike product of the dashing out of the Adamic eye of reason by the serpent.

In this sense, Taylor seeks to unwind the Satanic coil of postlapsarian language, which (as Bradford discovered with the word *necessity*) seems in the temporal world to "untwist . . . sacred bonds," particularly the bond between the straightforward (unfolded) human word and the disclosure (unfolding) of the Logos. He desires to unroll the sheet of history and of his life so that he will have something unscrolled to write upon, some *ground* to set his metrical feet upon. Just as the hidden divine promise of resolving balanced accounts is concealed within the apparent surface entanglements of human history, the circular and integrative balancing of his own account beneath the surface of the entangled language of his poem is what really matters to Taylor. Because this method is modeled after God's own practice of intertwining eternal denotation and temporal connotations, Taylor hopes his version of it in the logogic crux of his emblematic meditation will appeal to Him. In this way, the poet suggests subtly and hopefully that with so much intrinsic ability already, he might make a particularly good choice for the deity to elect.

At the surface level of his meditation Taylor unfolds (discloses, as in Genesis) the fallen world in serpentine bondage and, as well, beneath this surface of his meditation unfolds (predicts, as in Revelation) the disempowerment (uncoiling) of the bounds of the great dragon. Primarily Taylor manages his hope-giving balanced (circular) account in "Meditation 1.19" by organizing his poem around a recurrent emblem, the inversion of the figure of the arch used in "Meditation 1.8." The pit of an open grave filling up with water suggests the sea (deep) as a craterlike grave for the sun (Son); in turn this watery declivity suggests a pouchlike stomach, with decomposing juices and parasites, in the earth; and this image in turn suggests that the grave is the gateway to the pit of hell (at the center of the earth) or, more precisely, hell's mouth, the mouth of the serpentine great dragon of Revelation. This recurrent emblem imparts a denotative cohesion to "Meditation 1.19," and it provides the integrative center for the mutually constitutive themes and images of the poem: specifically the images of the great dragon (serpent, devil), the grave (death), darkness, and the deep, and, as well, the allusions to Hercules's donning a lion's skin to defeat the evil giants (rebellious sons of God), to slay the dragon/serpent, and to harrow Hades.

As this complex and remarkable concealed aesthetic design in "Meditation 1.19" indicates, Taylor was certainly interested in disclosing emblems (actually fashioning them, in our twentieth-century view). In no sense can his management of the inverted arch in this poem be read as an unenergetic rehearsal of a worn-out pattern lacking in tension. Nor can the imagery rooted in this aesthetic design be dismissed as rapid proliferations, free-associative in nature rather than coherent in design. Nor should the imagery in this poem be read merely as a form of "sport[ing] with drastically incongruent ways of naming."[50] The aesthetic design of "Meditation 1.19" is the work of Edward Taylor, a poet nervously hesitating over and playing at the logogic site where eternal definition and temporal meanings (the corrupted dispersion of divine denotation) intertwine. Like Bradstreet, Taylor knew that the function of the art of a humble poet is not to construct a maypole-like monument or a Tower of Babel representing the artist's prideful self-idolatry, but to conceal human art: to disguise human artfulness by revealing within it the hidden definitive (emblematic) artistry of the Logos. This is the poet we have yet to appreciate even after more than fifty years of having encountered his verse. Although Taylor in "Meditation 1.19" and Bradstreet in "Contemplations" penned their intricate poems for the attention of the divine mind, does this intention excuse us, as literary critics, from the perhaps Herculean labor of encountering their meditations as artistic texts designed, like emblems, to be *read*?

3

Laughter and Death

Because the logogic crux was for the Puritan author, as we have seen in the previous chapter, a site of a nervous meditative apprehension of human corruption and deific perfection, it sometimes became a place for reverent laughter or for reflective mourning. The Puritan author found authority for humor primarily in the Renaissance valuation of language as individualistic expression, though this authority (as we noted in the first chapter) was modified by certain Reformed and Augustinian notions.[1] The Puritan author found authority for mourning primarily in the Reformed authorization of language as an allegorical instrument revealing divine truth, although this authority (as we also remarked in the first chapter) is clearly likewise of Renaissance origin. In both instances, however, the humorous or elegiac writings of early Puritan American authors feature logogic cruxes similar to those characteristic of meditative verse. Moreover, these instances of laughter or mourning demonstrate how the logogic crux was not limited to personal meditation, but could also be informed by a larger political or social function.

In such works as Nathaniel Ward's satire and Urian Oakes's elegy, laughter and mourning are not mutually exclusive modes of expression. In fact, the two modes can fuse whenever Ward and Oakes anxiously manage them as a logogic crux where the temporal artistry of the author and the eternal art of God intertwine. This intersection prevents the monuments of their artistry from becoming a Mortonian maypole-like text, which (to apply Bradford's perspective) employs celebratory frivolity and solemnized depossession in order to idolize the secular self in a secular world; rather, Ward's and Oakes's artistry is redefined as a *memorial*, a communal site of joy and sorrow that recalls the human connection with God through the Logos. In this context, both authors emphasize the image of marriage and the family as a logogic site where historical and allegorical meanings combine in a manner similar to the function of the emblem of the cross for Bradstreet and the emblem of the inverted arch for Taylor.

All in Jest
Nathaniel Ward's The Simple Cobler

Although Nathaniel Ward's *The Simple Cobler of Aggawam in America* (1647) is as quaint and peculiar as modern readers have found it,[2] it has received very little attention from literary scholars.[3] This evasion is all the more surprising given the accuracy of an observation, made over thirty years ago, that specifically the vocabulary, the language, of Ward's odd little volume deserves careful scrutiny.[4] In fact, the extremely evident absence of any apparent overt structure in Ward's book, leading its critics to decry his apparent tendency to digress at will, all the more calls attention to the author's language as the only foothold the reader has, like it or not. That language, moreover, is downright bizarre, not only archaic and enmeshed in distorted English syntax but also inconsistent in narrative voice and in spellings, as if to elicit multiple interpretations from the reader. The language of Ward's text seems a veritable chaos occluding any clear meaning.

However, before one rushes to the conclusion that Ward must be one more representative of the American Puritan primitive artist,[5] the examples of Bradstreet and Taylor, also sometimes dismissed with this sobriquet, should be recalled. Just as Bradstreet and Taylor fashioned logogic sites where the external disorder of the postlapsarian temporal world intertwines with a concealed emblem of divine order, so too did Ward, who was a very learned minister famed during his life for his wit and his sermons. Both of these talents required a cogent management of language, and indeed Ward's other published writings reveal that the ostensibly "primitive" use of language in *The Simple Cobler* is intentional, possibly a logogic crux for the reader's contemplation.

One such site for the reader's puzzlement occurs in the closing lines of the last authorized edition of Ward's book. The placement of this peculiar expression especially calls attention to Ward's effort to direct his reader's attention to his words, where the reader should hesitate over the author's reverent play. Ward's final comment reads:

> And farewell simple world,
> If thou'lt thy Cranium mend,
> There is my Last and All,
> And a Shoem-Akers
> END.[6]

The mere peculiar appearance of the word *Shoem-Aker* demands attention from the reader. Obviously if it is read as if it were not a word peculiarly fissured, the expression means *shoemaker*, a sense reinforcing the puns on *last* and *all* in the stanza. But the word *is* fissured. Ward's curious sectioning of the word, the penultimate expression in his book, insistently intrudes upon the reader's attention. The fragmentation of this word resists the reader's desire to resolve its meaning as *shoemaker* because the capitalization of its second component intimates some other *concealed* sense as well.

To decode this sense, we need to consider some facts about Ward. From what external biographical evidence is available to us as well as from what internal textual evidence surfaces in his work, we can deduce that Ward's extensive education included a knowledge of several languages. He may have known French (hence the pun on Parliament/*Parlee-ment* [p. 52]) and Classical Greek (hence the pun on his own name, Theodore de la Guard [p. 3]). Like many other Puritan ministers of his time, Ward doubtlessly studied Latin and Hebrew.[7] He had, furthermore, some acquaintance with Dutch, if not only from his father's stay in Holland, then from his own apparent sojourn there sometime between 1620-1623.[8]

Such considerations are pertinent because the strange-looking word *Shoem-Aker* is a trilingual pun combining words from Hebrew and Dutch with the English word *shoemaker*. *Shoem* represents the sound of a Hebrew phoneme that means "little nothing" or "nothing."[9] *Aker* derives from the Dutch *egger*, which refers to one who harrows an acre for sowing. *Aker* also appears in the expression *waaregger* (from the Middle Dutch *wijsseggher*), which refers to a soothsayer. A combination of these meanings in *Shoem-Aker* characterizes Ward's narrator as the harrower or wise speaker of little nothings, a play on the word *wiseacre* (sometimes *wiseaker*), which in the seventeenth century defines a person who pretends to be wise.

This trilingual pun is a logogic site where surface verbal chaos (representing competing temporal connotations) coalesces with concealed verbal order (representing integrative eternal denotation). Reflecting the intersection of human wit and divine wisdom, this pun bids Ward's audience to read below the surface of the book in hand as they should read below the surface of historical events. Concerning the book in hand, the word *Shoem-Aker* serves as a seemingly frivolous moment, an experience of fissured temporality (as the bifurcated, distorted word suggests), when a hint of some concealed solemn underlying order is revealed. The reader must become, to apply contemporary metaphors, a sleuth or an archeologist delving into this mysterious logogic site where evident jocular verbal caprice and intimated somber message merge.

The reader who detects the puns in *Shoem-Aker* might, for instance, recall that the narrator has spoken of himself not only as a cobbler but also as a farmer and as a fool. Likewise, references to farming occur everywhere in the little volume. Two especially relevant passages read: "My last, but not least feare, is, That God will hardly replant his Gospel in any part of Christendome, in so faire an Edition as is expected, till the whole field hath been so ploughed and harrowed, that the soile be throughly cleansed and fitted for new seed"; "If men will needs gather Churches out of the world (as they say) let them first plough the world, sow it, and reap it with their own hands, and the Lord give them a liberall Harvest" (pp. 38, 41).

The cobbler speaks throughout his narrative not only of farming but also of various kinds of "ignorance" (p. 32). He archly refers to himself at various points as "simple," as "the universall Ideot of the world," as "the unablest adviser of a thousand, the unworthiest of ten thousand" (pp. 6, 14, 31). Badgering King Charles I about his opposition to Parliament, the narrator says that surely the monarch "is not *Charles le simple*," and he proffers "a simple supposall" which begins, "Were I a King . . ." (pp. 47, 59). As the title of his book suggests, the word *simple* itself is a locus of ambiguous meaning, including such definitions as *humble, insignificant,* and *foolish.*

Confusion, at the connotative level, continues when early in his narrative the cobbler explains *"When States dishelv'd are, and Lawes untwist, / Wise men keep their tongues, fools speak what they list"* (p. 31). At the temporal verbal site corrupt meanings intertwine with divine denotation, for in the postlapsarian world (as Bradford's conceit of the winding serpent also suggests) "Sathan . . . loves to fish in royled waters" (p. 5), not only within perverted royalty but also within twisted rhetoric. Consequently, in such a roiled world reversals of role, of definition, may be necessary. So the narrator facetiously suggests that he and the King switch roles. The narrator knows the truth of the quotation he cites from one of Horace's *Odes:* "*Misce stultitiam Consiliis brevem / —Dulce est desipere in loco*" (p. 72). Sometimes the wise act like fools, and sometimes acting fools are truly wise. In this instance, similar to Bradstreet and Taylor, Ward mingles Classical (secular) and biblical (divine) epigram; in fact, his authority to cite from Horace here derives from St. Paul: "If any man amonst you seeme to bee wise in this world, let him be a foole, that hee may be wise" (I Cor. 3:18). This Pauline/Horatian echo in Ward's book instructs the reader to look beneath the mere surface appearances of everything in the distorted world, including the surface of the narrator's conflicting disguises and his chaotic language.

In this sense, *Shoem-Aker* is a logogic crux suggesting that the narrator is a wise fool who, also like a farmer, harrows minds (especially the King's) in preparation for the seeds of truth contained in his book. On the one hand, this logogic site reflects once more the Bablic dispersion of meaning in the postlapsarian world that is suggested (as in Taylor's example as well) in the absence of enduring surface structure and in the prevalence of polysemous lingual play throughout *The Simple Cobler*. These external features of Ward's book conform to the narrator's sense of the temporal world as "royled," "*dishelv'd*," and "distract[ed]" (pp. 5, 31, 45), images recalling Bradford's perception of "the mutable things of this unstable world." On the other hand, this logogic site covertly integrates (*twists together*) two strands of seemingly unrelated and random references in the book, the farmer and the fool, to suggest that the narrative voice, like all human language, potentially conceals a coherent underlying divine design. Just as, for Puritans like Ward, the chaos of historical human experience in the world evinces from within a cohesive divine emblematical pattern, so too does the frenetic language of Ward's allegorical text reflecting that world. This very dualism is the art concealed in Ward's art, as suggested by the logogic crux of *Shoem-Aker*, which at once jocularly and solemnly urges the reader to look for a hidden design beneath the surface chaos of Ward's book.

The covert design of Ward's *The Simple Cobler* is much more extensive than this single logogic crux suggests,[10] and much more dire than the humor of its surface vehicle immediately indicates. As we noted in passing, Ward directs his narrator's puzzling discourse toward all Christians, but especially toward King Charles I, who was on the losing end of the Puritan revolution in England when *The Simple Cobler* was written. Ward creates a narrator who plays the role of a court jester, who also plays the role of a court advisor, and who also briefly plays the role of King Charles himself. The confusion of these shifts in role expresses Ward's homeopathic sense of the need for "distracting Remedies" in a "*dishelv'd State*" where "*Lawes untwist*" (pp. 31, 45) because distracted King Charles has temporarily forgotten the divine design.

Besides *Shoem-Aker*, other logogic cruxes occur in Ward's book where the reader, especially the King, might glimpse this concealed religiopolitical message about God's hidden design, in the world and in Ward's language. One strand of these sites derives from the motif of a proper marriage in Ward's book. In Puritan theology marriage may have lost its status as a liturgical sacrament, but in the Puritan mind the result of marriage, the family, was accorded communal sacramental status. This sense informed (as noted in chapter 1) Bradford's indictment of his fellow colonists for departing from the societal family. For the Puritans marriage symbolized a nexus linking secular and divine meaning that imaged the union of Christ and the elect, especially as understood in terms of the Song of Solomon.[11] Marriage and the family, then, were related Puritan symbols readily available to Ward, who shared his peers' notion that the most essential characteristic of this union was fidelity.[12]

References to marriage are scattered throughout *The Simple Cobler*. They are dispersed, the way allusions to farming and foolishness are scattered, in order to connote the nature of postlapsarian reality when perceived superficially. But just as the allusions to farming and foolishness participate in an underlying integrative pattern of definition, so do the seemingly random numerous references to marriage. In *The Simple Cobler* a proper marriage is the concealed divine paradigm, the seed of truth, that the wise-fool narrator tries to cultivate and reveal (from below) through his farmerlike harrowing of the surface of the times, of human attitudes (especially the King's), and of his own and others' words.

Ward's narrator, for example, attacks toleration specifically in terms of marital fidelity to truth. In one place he admonishes, "hee that would not lay down his money, his lust . . . while he might have had it; will tell his own heart, he plaid the very ill husband" (p. 10). In another place he combines this image of fidelity to truth in the marriage bed with his allusions to farming the seeds of truth: "The bed of Truth is green all the yeare long. Hee that canot solace himselfe with any saving truth, as affectionately as at the first acquaintance with it, hath not only a fastidious, but an adulterous heart" (p. 23). Such behavior amounts to "wanton fearlessenesse," "prophane prostitutions," "Poly-piety" rather than monogamy (pp. 8, 23,

46). In short, "Thy heart, saith the Prophet *Ezek.* 16.30. is weake, like the heart of an imperious whorish woman . . . ; alas, shee is hen-hearted, shee dares not look Truth in the face; if she dared, shee would neither bee whorish, nor imperious, nor weake" (p. 64).

Ward's narrator scatters hints of the consequences of this infidelity to truth by means of imagery suggesting bastard progeny. The result of "midwif[ing] out some ungracious Toleration," he indicates, is "most untimely births" and "squintey'd, wry-necked, and brasen-faced Errours" (pp. 6, 8, 22). In a similar vein, "to purloin from godly Ministers the first born of their fervent prayers and faithful preachings"—their fidelity to truth—is to encourage "wives without honesty" and "children without morality" (pp. 41, 66).

In contrast, the progeny of a marriage characterized by a fidelity to truth are like the harvests of successful farming: "If a Christian would picke out a way to thrive in grace," let him "make sure a blessing upon his Family, let him labour to multiply the Family of Christ, and beleeve, that he which soweth liberally, shall reape abundantly" (p. 41). The coalescence of the two strands of seemingly disparate allusions, marriage and farming, again intimates some underlying integrative divine pattern (truth) concealed within the "distracting" events of the reader's historical situation and within the "distracting" words of Ward's book, both faithful to divine truth. The choice is clear for Ward: either marry "One Truth in its purity," or, puns his narrator, "adulterate Truth" (p. 12).

In this way the narrator suggests the divine definition informing the image of a proper marriage. He also suggests a specific historical sense intertwined with this allegorical sense at the logogic site of the word *marriage*. This secular sense concerns, as it were, the marital relationship between England and New England. This feature of Ward's artistry emerges, for instance, when his narrator reveals that he has "been a solitary widdower almost twelve yeares" and has decided at the time he is penning his narrative "to make a step over to [his] Native Country for a yoke-fellow" (p. 27).[13] In other words, through his narrator's book Ward seeks to unite

New England and England in a proper marriage. His goal of uniting the two countries as spouses is announced by his persona: "I dare take upon me, to bee the Herauld of *New-England*" (p. 6). The problem is, however, that whereas New England is faithful to pure truth—adultery is hardly known there, he says (p. 58)—England has been shockingly *unfaithful*.

King Charles I is the source of this problem, in Ward's opinion, and so, as we noted earlier, one aim of his book is to harrow the unfaithful King's thoughts in order to replant the seeds of truth in the "bed" of his mind. Ward's narrator favors Puritan Parliament, in opposition to the King and the established church of England.[14] His charge against the King is adultery, an infidelity to truth that is symbolized in the King's "sinful mariage" to "*An Heretique* [for] *his Mate*" (pp. 55, 71).

Specifically the narrator refers here to Charles's marriage to Henrietta Maria of France, who was a Roman Catholic. He also refers to the King's defense of the high Anglican church, which in the Puritans' view seemed as tainted by Roman Catholicism as was Henrietta Maria, both encouraging the King to make "*the Pope his Christ*" (p. 71). He also refers to Charles's adulterous rejection of Puritanism, the pure yoke-fellow for a proper marriage by him. These historical definitions of the logogic crux represented in the image of marriage in *The Simple Cobler* are suffused, in Ward's opinion, with the underlying allegorical pattern of the divine marriage between Christ and the elect.

Just as the narrator's clever management of the wise, seemingly foolish cobbler and the foolish, seemingly wise monarch suggests how the divine and the temporal intertwine, his portrait of the King also involves reversed roles. Charles represents masculine authority, whereas his Puritan subjects represent his faithful spouse. But as a result of his perverted marriage, he becomes effeminate, which makes it necessary for his rightful yoke-fellow of New England (a metonymy for all Puritans at home or abroad) to break away from wifely submission and to assume the husband's authoritative role.

At the present moment, the cobbler asserts, the King possesses "the heart of an imperious whorish woman" (p. 64). In adulterating truth, he inverts the biblically defined hierarchical authority of husband over wife and thereby loses his imperial masculine authority over his feminine subjects. This inversion reminds the narrator of Adam's choice of Eve over divine truth at the time of the Fall. The narrator plays with the idea that the King might have become "Effeminate" as a result of his Adamlike devotion to his heretic wife and her encouragement of religious toleration: "to be a little Uxorious personally, is a vertuous vice in Oeconomicks; but Royally, a vitious vertue in Politicks" (p. 60):

> He cannot rule a Land,
> As Lands should ruled been,
> That lets himself be rul'd
> By a ruling Romane Queen   (p. 71)

Instead of maintaining authority over his wife, who in Puritan custom was to submit in total obedience to her husband,[15] Charles has surrendered to Henrietta Maria his patriarchal headship over the family of his subjects. With this idea in mind, the narrator admonishes, "It stands not with our Queens honour to weare an Apron, much lesse her Husband, in the strings" (p. 60).

Since King Charles is no longer the fatherly master of his family, his lack of fidelity, his *adulteration* of truth, has ramifications within his proper household. The narrator asks, "Shall the cheife bearing wombe of your Kingdome, be ever so constituted, that it cannot be delivered of its owne deliverance, in what pangs soever it be, without the will of one manmidwife, and such a man as will come and not come, but as he list: nor bring a Parliament to bed of a well-begotten Liberty without an entire Subsidy?" (p. 53). Not only does the King, in these terms, perversely insist upon a fee, as if his spouse (pregnant with truth) were a whore, but he also inappropriately plays at being a female, specifically a midwife who perversely will not assist in the birth of truth.

Moreover, the King is now surrounded by subjects who evidence his effeminate abdication of masculine authority as the head of the English household, as defined by eternal truth. The men of his court effeminately sport long hair, which detail the narrator interprets in terms of Paul's comment in I Corinthians 11.14-15. Paul says, in the Geneva version, "Doeth not nature it self teache you, that if a man haue long heere, it is a shame vnto him? But if a woman haue long heere, it is a praise vnto her." Moreover, if the men of his court reflect the King's inversion of his position as a male, the women of his court reflect the dominance of his Queen, whose Roman Catholic tastes authorize the fashions of courtly dress. Whereas in New England women wear "wife-worne Commons," in the English court women imitate "what dresse the Queen is in this week," clothing that symbolizes the rampant "loose tongued Liberty" (a looseness in several senses) of the court (pp. 25, 26, 28). When the narrator denounces the transformation of the women of the royal court into "surcingled and debauched"[16] (loose) "French flurts"[17] who are "imprisoned in French Cages, peering out of their hood-holes"[18] (pp. 26, 27), he indicates that the Roman Catholic influence evident in the fashions of the court implies that the Queen has displaced the King's authority there. The Queen, in the narrator's opinion, should be only a subservient wife, not a representative of the Whore of Babylon (the Roman Catholic Church), whose undue influence has not only made the uxorious King and the males of the court effeminate but also has made the women of the court whorishly loose in dress, speech, and behavior.

As the logogic site provided by the imagery of marriage shows, Ward's narrator plays two antithetical roles simultaneously: the foolish court jester and the wise court advisor, whose overt humorously twisted rhetoric fuses with covert sober absolute truth. Beneath the humor of *The Simple Cobler* lurk very dire implications. The book mentions "warre at home" (p. 51), discord in the family as a result of Charles's lack of fidelity. The narrator prefers a familial role, "onely [to] speak a word of Love," but he will play the rebellious sibling if necessary: "Doe you not foresee, into what importable head-tearings and heart-searchings you will be ingulfed, when the Parliament shall give you a mate, though but a Stale?" (pp. 17, 54). The word *stale* in Ward's time conveys several related ominous meanings: a deadlock (stale mate) in a game of chess between the King and the Puritan Parliament, a prostitute (what Parliament seems to be in the King's opinion when he requires a subsidy), and a fixed position of a body of armed men (the army of Parliament). These references to prostitution and warfare suggest an inversion of the household interaction between the King as husband and the Puritans as wife, an inversion that could lead to a divorce rather than a reunion. This possibility defines the darker meaning of the logogic crux. Just as the emblem of the "wracking" cross in Bradstreet's poem marks the intersection of possible redemption or possible destruction, so too Ward's image of marriage includes the possibility of an ideal union and, as well, the possibility of family strife eventuating in divorce. This latter potentiality especially expresses the threat beneath the narrator's humor, for in Puritan society divorce was possible if one of the married partners committed adultery.[19]

As we have seen, the King is faulted by the narrator for his adulteration of truth, for his lack of fidelity to his marriage to truth, for having "plaid the very ill husband." The possibility of divorce, moreover, becomes even more ominous when it is recalled that adultery is considered a capital crime in New England's *Body of Liberties*, which was largely written by Ward.[20] In the New England Puritan colonies, in fact, some people were actually hanged for this capital offense.[21] The indictment of the King on the charge of infidelity is finally a serious one. Through his wise-fool narrator, Ward warns the King about the possible fatal consequence—a permanent divorce not only from New England but also from his own life—if he fails to respond to the underlying design of divine truth, as soberly revealed within the seemingly Bablic humor of Ward's book.

Ward sent the king a copy of his book, a Trojan horse (like Morton's *New English Canaan*) with a treasonous threat concealed within. Apparently the Puritan belief, as expressed by Richard Mather, that the function of art is to conceal art had its political uses too, at least as evidenced by Ward's personally dangerous message in *The Simple Cobler*. Did Charles ever read

Ward's book? If he read it, did he laugh? If so, was his laughter un-Puritan: that is, was it laughter at the logogic site without any sense of the somber denotative underside of its humorous Bablic connotations? We do not know whether the king read *The Simple Cobler* and perceived what Ward might have meant by a book apparently written in jest. We do know that he did not achieve the marriagelike union between authority (the Monarchy) and truth (the Puritans) that Ward urged on him. And we know that he lost his head in 1649, less than two years after the publication of *The Simple Cobler.* If he had read Ward's book and jokingly scoffed at its covert message (the secular threat to the king's life and the religious plea to the king's mind), he would in effect have laughed himself to death.

Dissolving Stones
Urian Oakes's Elegy on Thomas Shepard

If Nathaniel Ward conceals the threat of death in the artistic wit of *The Simple Cobler,* Urian Oakes conceals the play of wit in the artistic mourning of *An Elegie upon That Reverend, Learned, Eminently Pious, and Singularly Accomplished Divine, My Ever Honoured Brother Mr. Thomas Shepard* (1677). Oakes was a minister as celebrated for his capacity for humor as was Ward a generation earlier. Although Oakes says that on this occasion of mourning "Wit avails not, when th' Heart's like to break," he subdues humor rather than abandons it, when, as a typical example, he indicates that his "Lesson's hard"—difficult to bear as well as difficult to convey.[22] Similar to Ward's management of the emblematical image of the ideal marriage as a logogic site where historical and anagogic meanings intermingle, Oakes likewise emphasizes in his elegy the ideal family as a radical nexus. For Oakes, the image of the father and his family, representing as well the relation between the soul and the body, and between the minister and the laity, serves as a logogic crux where his reader might contemplate the Christlike intersection of the divine and the temporal.

Oakes's indication of his purpose to set "eyes abroach, dissolve a stone" (p. 210) contributes to a development of this site.

Coming upon this passage, Oakes's audience would have readily decoded these virtually clichéd images as references to the eye of reason and to the stony heart. Reason and will—the will was readily imaged as the heart in Oakes's time—comprised the two chief faculties of the soul, as the Puritans understood it. Like Ward's objective with King Charles, Oakes's apparent goal is to use a form of wit (subdued humor in his elegy) to arouse and enlighten the reason of his audience and then to facilitate a change of heart in this audience, a change similar to the "turning of the heart" that was the crucial stage in the Puritan conversion process.[23]

To achieve this purpose, Oakes depicts the Puritan community as if it were a collective self comprised of soul and body.[24] In his elegy he draws a correspondence between Thomas Shepard's function as a spiritual father of the Puritan family and Shepard's similar function as a soul-like spiritual principle animating the collective body of the laity. In Puritan thought and in their gravestone designs, the soul was likened to the sun; like the sun, the soul prevents matter from remaining inert. Deceased Shepard, appropriately, is imaged as a fallen sun whose light has been extinguished (p. 212), an association also evident in Taylor's elegiac "Meditation 1.19."[25] Now Shepard's Puritan community is "Sublunary prey" in a darkened world forboding the inertia of death (p. 217). In this sense, the decease of Shepard is identical to the departure of the sunlike animating soul from the now lifeless body of the Puritan community. As Oakes wittily grieves, " "Our's now indeed's a lifeless *Corporation* / The Soul is fled, that gave it *Animation*" (p. 218).

While Shepard was the "very Soul" of his parish (corporation, body [*corpus*]) at Charlestown (p. 218), he served (like other Puritan ministers) as its reason and will—the two components of every human soul. As long as Charlestown, and by extension in the poem all Puritan communities, accepted guidance from such ministers as Shepard, New England allegorically reflected the regenerative state projected for the saint, in whom the soul would govern the body as it once did individually in Adam and collectively in the Edenic family of Adam and Eve.

Oakes also atomizes the soul into its two components, reason and will, in speaking of Shepard as the *head* of the Puritan family. Shepard specifically represented the rational element of his community: "solid Judgement, Pregnant Parts, / A piercing Wit" (p. 214).[26] In analogizing Shepard's death to the loss of sight, Oakes wittily plays not only on the motif of the minister's death as a loss of sunlight but also on the motif of the function of reason as the eye of the soul (an utterly conventional Puritan image). Similarly, Shepard is identified with the other component of the soul, the will (heart). The death of this man of "Large . . . Heart" (p. 216) "wounds both Head [reason] and Heart [will]," but is especially a "Heart-plague" (a loss of this faculty; a source for mourning) for New England (p. 220). He had attracted the "very Hearts" of those who knew him (p. 213), not only in the sense of their affection but more importantly in terms of their conversion (the turning of the heart). Particularly "in many a gratefull Breast" of these converted laity does the memory of Shepard remain, a memory like "a Monument" (p. 211).

In these saints there is a restored harmony between soul and body, between the heavenly order and the material order. The saints themselves are in a sense Christlike sons of God integrating temporal meaning and eternal definition. And, Oakes's elegy indicates, as long as New England submits as a familial body of believers to the fatherly soul principle of ministers, the possibility of this intersection of the eternal and the historical will specially exist for their community. Until the death of Shepard this possibility had been in evidence as a temporary reprieve from the fundamental fracture of the fall, as if a treaty between the order of heaven and the order of nature had been in effect (p. 213). In Shepard himself, as well, there was evidence of this reprieve in such signs as his ministerial expression of harmony, equilibrium, and moderation (p. 215). Shepard's example represented the intersection of "Art, Nature, Grace" (p. 213).

Specifically, Shepard's ministerial art (principally verbal expression) served as a nexus for nature and grace, even as the Puritan individual self and collective self are loci for the junction of the human (body) and the divine (soul). With this sense in mind, a sense particularly operative in his use of the image of the family as a logogic site, Oakes appropriately emphasizes mediation in his elegy. Whereas Christ, the Son/sun of God, served as a priest who mediated temporal experience heavenward for the elect, Shepard, the ministerial son/sun of God, served as a prophet who mediated eternal meaning earthward to the elect (p. 219). In this prophetic mediatory role of "Ambassador" (p. 213), Shepard was like a Leonidas at Thermopylae, "The man that stood i' th' gap, to keep the pass" (p. 212). Shepard's life as a minister had spanned the postlapsarian bifurcation between the body and the soul in the individual and in the collective self. Precisely analogous to his life, in Oakes's opinion, Shepard's ministerial verbal art bridged the postlapsarian fundamental fracture between temporal connotative meanings and eternal denotative definition, the very bifurcation rhetorically stressed by Satan in Taylor's *Gods Determinations*.

Shepard was "Pow'erful i' th' *Pulpit*, and sweet in converse, / To weak ones gentle, to th' Profane a Terrour" (p. 217). His ministerial words typically mirrored the ideal internal harmony between reason and will in the individual and in the collective self: "His Words were few, well season'd, wisely weigh'd / And in his Tongue the Law of Kindness sway'd" (p. 215). In prophetically mediating wisdom and love for his laity he *wisely* and *kindly* served as their soul principle of reason (relishing wisdom) and will (relishing love), and related them, as a temporal body (*corporation*), to eternal definition.

If Shepard's ministerial life and verbal art were in effect, according to Oakes, logogic sites mediating the postlapsarian gap between heaven and nature, so is Oakes's elegy. Oakes is a minister too, and the muted wit of his "Elegiack Knell," authorized by David's example in the Psalms (p. 208), plays at the possibility of his own and the Puritan community's recovery from the present condition, in which "Wit avails not" because "th' Heart's like to break" (p. 210). In fact, as we shall see, Oakes's wit (reason) resuscitates, tries to be of service in the poem by playing further at, the logogic site imaged in the family; for him the family is a paradigm for the relation between soul and body, and between minister and laity. Oakes will especially focus on the broken heart, the will, in this motif. In managing this logogic crux in his elegy Oakes takes on the Leonidasian role of Shepard as the man who stood in the gap between temporal experience and heavenly design.

In imitation of Shepard's sermonic technique (p. 217), Oakes speaks powerfully, integrating in his poem both gentleness (hope in the eternal) and terror (despair over the temporal). Oakes subdues his verbal cleverness and his humor in imitation of Shepard's concealment of his erudition. Such moderation is appropriate to their mutual aim of bridging the apparent gap between (by intimating the integration of) heaven and earth, soul and body, minister and laity, father and family. Only fettered verse (shackled feet, as it were) will serve (p. 208).[27] "No forc'd, affected, artificial Tone," no "Daring *Hyperboles*" (p. 210), will serve Oakes's assumption of Shepard's Christlike mediatorial function.

This mediatorial function is expressed in the elegy whenever the family motif and its correspondent imagery surface as logogic sites where the temporal event of Shepard's death is suffused with divine meaning. This mediatorial function is specifically addressed at a critical moment when Oakes raises a central question about whether his words can span the postlapsarian gap ("the pass") between heavenly design and earthly event, or whether they will not be in "time and measure" (in sufficient metrical harmony, as it were) to prevent something dire from coming to "pass" (p. 208):

> What! must we with our God, and Glory part?
> Lord! is thy Treaty with *New-England* come
> Thus to an end? and is War in thy Heart   (p. 213)

In other words, has the intersection of anagogic design and historic Puritan experience ended? Were that intersection to continue, then Oakes would be able to disinter his buried wit in the elegy because, then, hopeful joy would readily balance despairing grief. But identical to Ward's management of the marriage motif in *The Simple Cobler*, Oakes shows the intersection of the divine and the temporal in the family motif without resolving the question of whether at this point in their experience integration or bifurcation will prevail. For Oakes, either the Puritans will, individually (as soul and body) and collectively (as minister and laity), be a proper family again or they will not—the same sort of problem raised by Ward concerning the paternal authority of King Charles and the familial submission of New England. Threat and hope fuse at Ward's and Oakes's logogic sites, even as connotative meanings and denotative definition intertwine there. So Oakes leaves unanswered the question about whether God's treaty with New England has ended. The open question is a religiopolitical jeremiad instructing his audience to hesitate over the logogic site in his poem, there to consider the nature of their times. Through the subdued wit of its mediatorial language, particularly at the logogic crux of the family motif, Oakes demonstrates another example of the Puritan author's conviction, as stipulated by Richard Mather, that the function of art is to conceal art.

Oakes's artistic management of two specific images, associated with his use of the family motif in his elegy, summarizes particularly well the message and the manner of his deployment of the logogic crux. These images occur in the passage that states his aim to set "eyes abroach, dissolve a stone." We have seen how these references to the eye or reason and the will (heart) figure in a number of Oakes's artistic maneuvers in his elegy, but we also should detect one more integrative feature of his management of them.

The image of the will here recalls references to the stony heart that abound in scripture and in Puritan sermons to represent the unregenerate state of the will. This stoniness must be broken or else it will serve as a sort of tombstone to the spiritual death of the soul. The breaking of this stony heart, conversion, is what the minister hopes his agential prophetic mediatorial words will achieve through God's power. This was deceased Shepard's aim, with some success, according to Oakes; but now the whole force of Shepard's life, Oakes suggests, might serve as if it were a form of efficacious language similar to Shepard's sermons. Shepard's death is a potential occasion when "th' Heart's like to break" (p. 210). Even in his death, particularly as conveyed in the mediatorial force of Oakes's elegy on this death, there is one final opportunity for the Puritans of New England to experience a breaking of their stony hearts.

This shattering of the stony heart is like the removal of the rock at Christ's tomb. The breaking of the stony heart means the breakdown of the tombstone that marks one's existence only in the temporal terms of physical death. And this fact justifies Oakes's sense that to build such "Prophets Sepulchers" is "In vain" (p. 219); it is also *vain*, in the sense that the construction of such a monument, including the Bablic memorial of elegiac verse, is potentially a form of iconic idolatry. This is Bradstreet's point as well in "Contemplations," where she fractures the tombstonelike monument of her verse; and Oakes similarly fetters his grief with a repudiation of it as a prideful secular memorial: "Stop, stop my Pen! lest *Israel's* singer sweet / Should be condemn'd" (p. 208). Neither a sepulcher in a graveyard or in an elegy is needed, for the connotative meanings of these temporal icons become shattered when the stony heart, *vainly* cherishing them *in vain*, is broken. Then the denotative *memorial* "Monument" to Shepard (the true memory) will no longer be entombed within the "Breast," just as Christ is no longer hidden in the grave. And then Oakes's suppressed art of wit (intimating hopeful promise) will no longer need to be concealed within the tomb of his artful elegy (expressing dire threat).

This very intersection of dual possibilities is essentially featured in Oakes's management of the logogic crux. There, he hopes, his readers will hesitate, as if granted one more chance for their hearts to break, to dissolve, and then to reveal the true denotative memory buried within it. This image of dissolution is linked to the image of setting "eyes abroach." The eye of reason must be convicted or pierced by divine truth, something suggested in Oakes's reference to "piercing Wit," which as we noted refers to both Shepard and himself. This lanced eye of reason will pour forth tears of repentance and tears of joy, which will as it were fall on the rocky heart (will).

In focusing on this image of the pierced weeping eye and the dissolved stony heart Oakes essentially asks, and leaves unresolved, a question similar to the explicit one we noted of God's treaty with New England. He raises this question: is Shepard's death a blinding of the eye of reason and a breaking of the heart of the collective self of the Puritan community that leaves it in an eternal darkness signifying the withdrawal of the Son/sun of God; or is Shepard's death a piercing of the eye of reason and a dissolving of the heart of the Puritan collective self that will lead it further toward the fulfillment of their divine mission on earth? Bradford had arrived at a similar question as he pondered over the word *necessity*.

This question goes unanswered in Oakes's poem; the answer lies hidden in the heart of his audience. By dissolving the stony exterior of connotations to remind his audience of the concealed divine denotation at the heart of themselves and of their community, he only artistically manages the interactive imagery of his logogic site so that it conveys simultaneously two opposite meanings. And these antithetical meanings are apparently reinforced by scripture: whereas Isaiah 48:21 reports (in an adumbration of the saved Christian) how God cleaved the rock for the Israelites so that water gushed out to revive them, Numbers 20:7-12 reports Moses's disobedient act of striking instead of speaking to a rock, from which water did indeed flow but as a result of which Moses was denied entry into the Promised Land. Like these two biblical images of water coming from a rock, Oakes's use of the image of the pierced eye of reason flowing forth and dissolving the stony heart conveys two alternative meanings—one of threat, one of hope—concerning his Puritan reader both as an individual self (soul and body) and as a part of the collective self (minister and laity; father and family).

By combining jeremiad (threat) and wit (hope) together, just as Ward fused wisely foolish menace and humor, Oakes artistically manages the images of the weeping eye and the dissolving heart as features of the family motif, a mysterious crux where he and his Puritan readers might contemplate the intersection of human purpose and deific plan. What hope there is in Oakes's elegy, as in Ward's *The Simple Cobler*, resides in the fact that such logogic sites exist as ever-present *memorials* of the human connection with God through the Logos.

4

Breaking Verbal Icons

So far we have reviewed occasions when several seventeenth-century Puritan American writers tried to mediate the requirement to use language in celebration of the infinite wonder of divine artistry (Christ, nature, and history) and the inherent tendency of this language to become an iconic graven image of authorial self-idolatry. These writers fashioned logogic sites where they and their audience could hesitate and contemplate the potentiality of postlapsarian human language to reveal simultaneously both concealed authorial pride and concealed deific design. In the instances of Bradford's use of the word *necessity*, Mather's use of *art*, Taylor's use of *hand* and *balanced account*, Bradstreet's use of *wrack*, Ward's use of *marriage*, and Oakes's use of *family*, as we have seen, human language can serve the Puritan author as a possible theanthropic site where corrupt human definitions and pristine divine meanings intersect. This coalescence functions like the call of a typical Puritan sermon for the laity to consider the opportunity, the junction of choice, which predeterminatively exists for certain elect individuals. This coalescence of the temporal and the eternal reminds authors and readers alike of the threat of their damnation and, at the same time, of the promise of their redemption before God's denotative design. The unresolved dualism at the logogic crux ideally leaves the contemplator suspended between terror over this threat and joy over this promise.

In the eighteenth-century, Jonathan Edwards shares a similar notion of the instability of language at the logogic site, but with a difference from his New England predecessors. Edwards does not exploit the polysemous nature of words to intimate an all-encompassing divine denotation that might intrinsically inform such a plentitude of connotative meanings. On the contrary, he sometimes hints at the divinity concealed at the logogic crux by imploding this abundance and by obliterating the conventional connotations of words.

Not *all* of Edwards's imagery operates in this way, of course; many of his images perform simple analogical functions and remain unvexed by a complicating self-reflexivity. Even in this mode of presentation, however, Edwards's imagery is designed to arouse uncomfortable emotional reactions in an audience.[1] More dramatically, on other occasions, Edwards strategically singles out a logogic site and manages it in terms of a self-reflexive minimalism that approaches an eschatological erasure of the word. This artistic procedure, a form of iconoclastic breaking of verbal images, possibly leveled whatever connotative rational expectations Edwards's eighteenth-century New England Puritan audience might have routinely, comfortably associated with the word under assault.

Nature, Reason, and Language
Jonathan Edwards in Reaction

Edwards is a troubling figure for a critic. His private life is particularly shrouded, and his public life and writings represent a melange of views. One component of this puzzle surfaces in the critical debate over whether he was modern or conservative in his outlook.[2] In this debate, so much depends on the critic's specific area of focus. In the areas most pertinent to my study, I find that Edwards may have appreciated much of the learning of his day, but that increasingly he expressed a relish for the erstwhile beliefs and ways of the first generation of the Puritans in America. In this regard, to label Edwards as "the last medieval American—at least among the intellectuals," goes too far;[3] but it is fair to note that he often derived authority (and perhaps personal inspiration) in his major work, such as *A Treatise Concerning Religious Affections* (1746), from such early Puritan divines as William Ames and Thomas Shepard, for example.[4] Moreover, his final break with his liberalized Presbyterian congregation at Northampton was catalyzed by his declared intent to restrict the Lord's Supper to church members, to require a spiritual relation before admission to the church, and even to end automatic baptism for the newborn of the community—all features of Puritanism a century earlier in New England.[5] Edwards, then, is particularly eligible for the sobriquet *Puritan* when we consider this conservative cast of his mind as well as his eighteenth-century defense of such doctrines as justification before sanctification, the debilitating pervasiveness of original sin, and the absence of true virtue.

One component of this debate on the modernity and the conservatism of Edwards's thought is the question of his knowledge of the philosophy of John Locke. This issue remains another sensitive area in critical debates about Edwards. It is reasonable to suspect that Edwards knew something of Locke's arguments,[6] but, I think, caution is in order before concluding that he was Lockean in any fundamental sense.[7] In many ways, in fact, Edwards seems more committed intellectually to philosophical idealism. He considered the material world to be a representation of the divine mind, and he understood human ideas to be the product of the mind (the divine image) rather than only the result of sensorial perceptions. For Edwards, finally, there is no ontological identity in material reality or in the human mind other than as the product of an arbitrary, creative idea in the divine mind.[8] Earlier Puritans, as the logogic sites in their writings indicate, had maintained an odd mixture of idealism and empiricism in their thinking. So did Edwards to some extent, but he tended to polarize toward the idealistic features of his thinking. This polarization had a profound impact on his handling of the traditional Puritan logogic crux in his early sermons.

Concerning language, Edwards opposed what he perceived as an emerging style in his time. On one occasion, for instance, he explicitly rejected "elegance of language" and "such ornaments as politeness and modishness of style" presently in vogue.[9] Rather, a distinctly old-fashioned emphasis on "method and order in [religious] discourses, for the help of understanding and memory," characterized Edwards's basic position, as stated in *Some Thoughts Concerning the Present Revival of Religion in New England* (1743).[10] Words for Edwards are ideally ministerial implements, their capacity for artfulness to be kept humbly and safely subservient to their divinely sanctioned utilitarian function. The human author's artistry as such is, in Edwards's opinion, worth nothing. This skeptical attitude is even more conservative than the ambivalence toward language evident in his New England predecessors.

Edwards's distrust of postlapsarian words ran so deep, in part, because he aligned human language with two modes of reference privileged by some thinkers in the eighteenth century: nature and reason. As we saw in the preceding chapters, reason and nature were treated with mixed feelings by seventeenth-century Puritan writers, but nature and reason had become elevated by a number of eighteenth-century thinkers as testaments to human capability.[11] This certainly occurred in the philosophy of John Locke, and it reached something of an apogee of implication when Thomas Paine observed (years after Edwards's death) that "the Almighty lecturer, by displaying the principles of science in the structure of the universe, has invited man to study and to imitation."[12]

Nature in this Deistic sense provides not only an empirical field of reference for scientific explanations of the meaning of existence but also a material field of reference for the meaning of human conduct (ethics). To benefit from this natural field, these eighteenth-century thinkers indicated, humanity need only apply reason, and indeed the quotation by Paine appears in a book he titled *The Age of Reason* (1794-1796). Although the early Puritans had from the start regarded reason as one of the two chief faculties of the soul (the divine image in every person), they had always carefully indicated that its postlapsarian capacities were much impeded. Puritan thinkers had always been concerned with establishing the limits of fallen reason at the same time as they were defining the areas in which this faculty had restricted competency.[13] But, as it were, the more emphatic Renaissance valorization of human reason was resurrected with new force in the eighteenth-century, when this faculty became, for some thinkers of the time, a privileged mode by which humanity could learn everything it needed to know from nature and thereby achieve a secular millennium for itself on earth.

Edwards had a special regard for nature. Of that there can be no doubt.[14] But despite his youthful empirical inquiries into nature, as in his derivative youthful essay "Of Insects,"[15] his adult approach to the natural world was one of respectful awe, not one of mastering its secrets. It was not as empirical fact that nature finally mattered to him, any more than it did ultimately to Anne Bradstreet in "Contemplations." For Edwards, nature was "a kind of voice or language of God to instruct intelligent beings in things pertaining to Himself."[16]

This instruction, however, is experienced by humanity as a mystery. In trying to decode the symbols of nature in order to detect their spiritual meanings—essentially a scripturally confirmed denotation—humanity must use its rational capacities.

But reason is insufficient, as even the early Puritans indicated, and so, as a result, for Edwards nature lures humanity to one supreme revelation: that whereas nature is not alienated from divine denotation, humanity is. This point is precisely identical to the observation made by Bradstreet in "Contemplations," for example, and precisely opposite to the claim made later by Paine in *The Age of Reason*. Edwards might have conceded, on the subject of postlapsarian reason at least, Locke's belief that knowledge of the material world in the human mind depends on sensory perceptions of that world (including nature) and on recollection; but for Edwards, any such dependence upon nature through corrupt reason dwarfs humanity's sense of itself rather than enhances its self-esteem. Nature, the art of the Logos, may in fact be a crux where the divine and the temporal intersect, but in Edwards's view during the 1730s, fallen humanity finds in nature less an elusive promise of regeneration (registered as awe in the viewer/

thinker) than a likely indictment for unregenerateness (registered as terror in the viewer/thinker). These two temporal connotations, suffused with cryptic divine denotation, occur in the polarities of Edwards's own response to nature; as he tells us in his "Personal Narrative" (c. 1739), nature could elicit uncommon "terror when [he] saw a thunder-storm rising" and could also elicit ineffable awe when his soul seemed like "a little white flower . . . low and humble on the ground, opening its blossom, to receive the pleasant beams of the sun's glory."[17]

It is important, however, to notice the obvious: that awe and terror are feelings, not rational reactions to nature. In stressing these nonempirical responses to nature, Edwards subtly suggests another mode of knowing different from the encounter of reason and nature celebrated by some of the religious and philosophical thinkers of his time. Edwards's mode of knowing through feeling does not anticipate the impulse of the Romantics, any more than does Anne Bradstreet's sense of nature, but actually (as we shall consider) reinstates a feature of earlier Puritan belief, another conservative element of Edwards's thought. Clues to this maneuver surface in *A Divine and Supernatural Light, Immediately Imparted to the Soul by the Spirit of God* (1734).

In this sermon Edwards asserts flatly that the encounter of reason and the natural world does not provide the best source of knowledge about the divine design, not even with scripture guiding the viewer's interpretative eye. "Men have a great deal of pleasure in human knowledge, in studies of natural things," Edwards writes, possibly recalling his own youthful interests and the proclivity of some of the thinkers of his time; "but this is nothing to that joy which arises from . . . divine light shining into the soul."[18] Here he again privileges a feeling (joy) over reason as he shifts the focus of discussion from the exterior world of nature to the interior world of the mind. This shift, informed by his idealist bent, occurs as well in "The True Christian's Life, A Journey Towards Heaven," a sermon also delivered in the early 1730s[19] that instructs Edwards's audience to take "a transient view" of "pleasant places, flowery meadows, or shady groves."[20] Turn within, Edwards teaches. In the mind, or soul, one may find influences of the natural world, but it is more important to find there, as well, the influences of the supernatural. Only the presence of supernatural grace resolves the mixed human response (awe and terror) to the dualistic connotative, temporal significance of nature as a reflection of the unitive denotative, eternal referent of God.

To support the idea of two kinds of knowing (one rational, the other affective) in *A Divine and Supernatural Light*, Edwards claims a distinction between two kinds of grace. There is common grace: "common grace only assists the faculties of the soul to do that more fully which they do by nature, as natural conscience or reason will, by mere nature, make a man sensible of guilt, and will accuse and condemn him when he has done amiss." By "natural conscience," "natural reason," and "ratiocination," Edwards means, simply, what earlier Puritans meant by *scientia*, which (as we noted in the preceding chapters) was one of the two modes of rationality possessed by Adam.

When Adam fell, he and humanity subsequently lost *sapientia* (an intuitive wisdom), which was hierarchically superior to and which contextualized *scientia* (knowledge through the senses). Postlapsarian humanity has limited access to knowledge of the material world and of the divine order through the operations of weakened *scientia*. However, the sensorial perceptions of *scientia* remain fundamentally occluded without the assistance of clarifying *sapiential* knowing. In covertly returning to this distinction, Edwards indicts those of his contemporaries who argue for the advancement of humanity in terms of the empirical encounter of human reason and nature. In Edwards's opinion, these eighteenth-century spokesmen are not wrong, in one sense: *scientia* is indeed a mode of knowing sanctified by common grace. But, Edwards admonishes, *scientia* was never sufficient to humanity's appreciation of the divine order, and in postlapsarian corrupted condition, it is even less adequate than it was in prelapsarian Adam. As he says in "Man's Natural Blindness in the Things of

Religion," "Of so little avail is human strength, or human reason and learning, as a remedy against the extreme blindness of the human mind. The blindness of the mind, or an inclination to delusion in things of religion, is so strong, that it will overcome the greatest learning, and the strongest natural reason."[21] Something else is needed, something outside of nature and natural reason (*scientia*).

Needed is the restoration of a mode of knowing similar to *sapientia* in Adam before the Fall. This is the province of special grace. If the influence of common grace on natural reason (*scientia*) is available fairly generally to humanity, special grace (restoring something of *sapientia*) is reserved for the elect, the predestined few chosen for salvation before the beginning of time by the deity. Special grace, Edwards explains in *A Divine and Supernatural Light*, "acts in the mind of a saint as an indwelling vital principle" that imparts "a new spiritual principle of life and action." Through special grace "not only are remaining [*sciential*] principles assisted to do their work more freely and fully, but those [*sapiential*] principles are restored that were utterly destroyed by the fall." It imparts "the most excellent knowledge of the angels, yea, of God himself," something intuitive and affective that cannot be truly apprehended by mere rational encounters with the natural world. As mysterious as light (Edwards's image), special grace is imparted by God "immediately, not making use of any intermediate natural causes, as he does in other knowledge." In other words, unlike *sciential* knowledge, *sapiential* wisdom is not dependent upon nor can be achieved through sensorial encounters with the natural world.

Edwards cedes, in effect, Locke's empiricist argument, but only concerning the function of *scientia*. For Edwards, however, *sciential* reason is a distorted form of knowing incapable of leading anyone to salvation, including the sort of redemption suggested by the eighteenth-century secular millennialism emerging during Edwards's life.[22] In a sense, Edwards here recovers the earliest Puritan understanding that "there is no greater ods in the world than betweene our owne reason and Gods wisedome," as English divine Richard Greenham typically explained to his sixteenth-century audience.[23] Edwards similarly takes the high ground, there to reclaim the hierarchically superior faculty of *sapientia* as the necessary faculty in the eventual restoration of the elect to their the prelapsarian Adamic state. This stress on two modes of knowing conforms to Edwards's idealism: that God's idea is the ontological basis of nature and that a sense of this denotative reality can only be experienced *sapientially* (affectively), not *scientially* (rationally), through the restorative efficacy of special grace in the saint. In a process which will be finalized only after the departure of the saint from the material world, special grace imparts a preliminary intuitive apprehension of the divine idea when, as Edwards says in *A Divine and Supernatural Light*, it "assimilates the nature [of the soul] to the divine nature, and changes the soul into an image of the same glory that is beheld."[24]

This review of Edwards's views on reason and nature, at least during the 1730s,[25] aids in an understanding of his convictions about language at that time. Edwards's disapproval of eighteenth-century stylistic embellishments, similar to the first-generation Puritans' rejection of rhetorical ornateness in high Anglican sermons, is linked to his repudiation of reason. Verbal art is a construction of the human mind, and it tends in the eighteenth century (from Edwards's perspective) to serve as an iconic monument pridefully valorizing reason and, by extension, all human endeavors. Because language readily expresses human vanity, it has, in Edwards's opinion, a very limited role in the process that most matters: the redemption of the soul. As *A Divine and Supernatural Light* indicates, God makes use of a minister's sermonic discourse, but if special grace is dispensed by the deity, it is not conveyed in or through human language, including the word of God: "The word of God is only made use of to convey to the mind the subject matter of this saving instruction: and this indeed it doth convey to us by natural force or influence." Just as "God makes use of . . . a good understanding, a rational brain," Edwards explains, "God makes use of means; but it is not as mediate causes to produce this effect" of special grace, and so "the word . . . is no proper cause of this effect," this immediate affective *sapiential* "sense of the heart." For Edwards, words are like nature: merely limited connotative *signs* of divine denotation. Since words operate "by natural force," they do not mediate in Christic fashion, and so do not participate in the suprarational illumination that they prophesy.

Apparently, Edwards does not hold a view of nature precisely similar to Bradstreet's, or of language at all similar to Taylor's. He does indicate, as we saw, that nature and language are designed for human instruction and that nature maintains a prelapsarian integrity; but he seems to lack Bradstreet's and Taylor's Augustinian sense of nature and language as similar expressions of the Logos that provide humanity with some sense of the proximity of the deity in the natural world. This difference is perhaps ironic insofar as Edwards sought to align himself with the beliefs and practices of the first generation of Puritans and in the process appears to have exceeded their conservatism. Edwards is oddly more narrowly Calvinistic than are Bradstreet and Taylor, who are closer to their Renaissance and high Anglican cultural roots in their understanding of nature, reason, and language.

In fact, Edwards's position on language in particular suggests a very reductive interpretation of the Calvinistic perception of the Lord's Supper. That seventeenth-century Puritans possessed a keen awareness of the sacramentality of the Lord's Supper is beyond question.[26] In Taylor's case, for instance, this perception of the Lord's Supper, the occasion for his *Preparatory Meditations*, neatly corresponds with his Augustinian heritage of viewing language as representative of the theanthropic nature of the Logos as Christ. Edwards, in contrast, evinces much less emotional intensity over the Lord's Supper and, aptly, less of the tradition of Augustine or the tradition of the Renaissance pertaining to the dual nature of language. Concerning language in the context of the eighteenth-century stress on reason and nature, Edwards aligns himself with a very strict reading of the Calvinistic celebration of the Lord's Supper, a reading by Edwards that derives more conservative implications from this sacrament than is characteristic for many first generation Puritans.

If we take Edwards at his word, he held a traditional Congregationalist view of the Lord's Supper from the very beginning of his ministry, and he had conformed to the liberal Presbyterian practices (including open admission) of his grandfather in Northampton with great skepticism. He makes this point in *An Humble Inquiry into the Rules of the Word of God Concerning the Qualifications Requisite to a Compleat Standing and Full Communion in the Visible Christian Church* (1749), which defends "the ways of our fathers" by arguing for the curtailment of open admission, a practice that (he thought) allowed for the possible sacrilege of the Lord's Supper. Because Edwards reclaims the earlier Puritan appreciation of this sacrament as a nonconverting ordinance, he also argues for the reestablishment of the communicant's interior preparation and insists on the propriety of a subsequent spiritual relation as two prerequisites to admission to the Lord's Supper if the sanctity of this sacrament is to be preserved. Edwards's understanding of the Lord's Supper, however, is more rigorously Calvinistic than these two features of his argument indicate.

For our purposes in this study, the one component of Calvin's teachings on the Lord's Supper that is most evident in Edwards's attitude toward words can be found in the concept of "spiritual communion." Calvin stresses a separation between the exterior sacramental signs (bread and wine) of the Lord's Supper and the interior efficacy of the Spirit. In contrast to the Roman Catholic doctrine of transubstantiation and the Lutheran doctrine of consubstantiation, Calvin indicates that the external elements of the sacrament remain utterly unchanged during the celebration of the Lord's Supper and serve merely as the instruments of grace, which is in no way whatsoever *essentially* bound to these material signs.

This view is identical to Edwards's attitude toward sermonic language, which (as we saw in *A Divine and Supernatural Light*) serves God as an instrument (a "natural force") of special grace without itself ever participating in that grace: "the word . . . is no proper cause of this effect," of this immediate affective *sapiential* "sense of the heart." For Edwards, words, merely a "natural force," are like the symbols of nature and the external sacramental elements of the Lord's Supper: restricted connotative signs of divine denotation that can never theanthropically fuse with the spiritual (suprarational) wisdom that they serve.

When Edwards speaks of the need for "method and order" in religious discourse, then, he emphasizes an elementary level of language, how it is like nature in utilitarianly instructing the *sciential* perceptions of humanity. But when Edwards indicates, in what at first might appear as a contradiction on the same page of *Some Thoughts*, that "an exceeding affectionate way of preaching" is capable of "a much greater tendency to beget true apprehensions" of "the great things of religion,"[27] he speaks of a higher function of limited language. These two remarks reflect a tension in Edwards's thought, torn between the older Puritan claims for order and method, and more recent post–Great Awakening claims for dynamic sermons. But, in an important sense, Edwards's advocacy of an affectionate way of preaching suggests a technique that might expose the hearer to a mode of perception beyond that of *sciential* order and method, to a mode of mental apprehension designatable as "rational" feeling, *sapiential* intuition. Even when thinking of this higher capacity of human words, Edwards remains critical of the limits of language because of its bond to *sciential* reason, specifically in Edwards's terminology, "natural reason."

If, in Edwards's opinion, human language proves inadequate to the communication of *sapiential* knowledge because of its relation to fallen human reason, its insufficiency also stems from its relation to the natural world. In his posthumously published "Dissertation Concerning the End for Which God Created the World" (1765), he specifically complains about "indistinctness and obscurity," about the "great imperfection of the expressions we use" concerning "those things that are divine," those things that evince an incomprehensible "sublimity."[28] This point is dramatized by the narrator of the "Personal Narrative" when he laments the failure of language to describe his religious experiences: "I know not how to express"; "what I felt within, I could not express"; "my wickedness, as I am in myself, has long appear'd to me perfectly ineffable."

A particularly pertinent moment occurs in *A Careful and Strict Enquiry into the Modern Prevailing Notions of That Freedom of the Will* (1754): "words were first formed to express external things; and those that are applied to express things internal and spiritual, are almost all borrowed, and used in a sort of figurative sense." In this passage Edwards (whether unwittingly or knowingly) agrees with Locke that words originate from the perceptions of the sensorium, although they rarely are as clear as the senses tend to be.[29] Here lies the core of Edwards's skepticism about language: human words depend on the external, the natural world. Thus bound to nature, the "natural force" of human language is profoundly limited to communication with "natural reason" *(scientia)*. As a result, Edwards remarks in *Freedom of the Will*, human language is "very deficient, in regard of terms to express precise truth," not only "concerning our own minds" but most especially the divine mind.[30]

This attitude toward language, as a "natural force" delimited (like the exterior sacramental signs of the Lord's Supper) by its bondage to "natural reason" and the natural world, informs Edwards's modification of the early Puritan tradition of exploiting words as potential logogic sites where connotative temporal meanings may conceal a denotative eternal definition. By severing the Renaissance and Augustinian roots of this early Puritan tradition, he reads his predecessors more conservatively than they themselves in fact were, at least concerning language. Like his Puritan ancestors, Edwards maintains an appreciation of the instability of language as a logogic crux, but in managing the ambiguity of this crux, he reveals its hidden divine denotation very differently from his New England predecessors. Rather than explore, in a nervous but exuberant artistry, the plentitude of various associational meanings at a logogic site, Edwards sometimes obliterates all rational and natural connotations. In this way he denies his audience the sort of security of identity they seek in language, just as they do in nature and in the processes of their own reason; and ideally, in Edwards's terms, they *rationally feel*, as he says in *God Glorified in the Work of Redemption* (1731), "emptied of . . . self" and totally dependent upon God's arbitrary will.[31]

When working in this mode, Edwards destroys the logogic site as if it were an idolatrous iconic image, as unreliable as are the "images and shadows" of everything else in the natural world and in "natural reason." Rather than an abundance of meanings, these Edwardsean logogic sites suggest an absence of reliable *sciential* meaning, a Barthesean *aporia* (as it were) leading to a lacuna or void intimating an unsayable, unimaginable ultimate definition receding infinitely before the pursuing human mind. Assaulting the self's illusion of integrity founded on reason and nature, on signs, this erasure of a word into vacuity expresses Edwards's sense of the inability of language to name Adamically, or *sapientially*. This procedure corresponds to Edwards's explicit comments on the inability of language (or sacramental signs of any kind) to participate in special grace, the restorer of something of this *sapientia* in the elect.

Edwards defends and uses "method and order," principally the structure of his sermons,[32] to communicate to his audience's rational faculty of *scientia*. But, as we also noted, he simultaneously defends and uses an "affectionate way of preaching," principally by means of the individual words in his sermons, to stimulate his audience's receptivity to *sapiential* apprehension, should God communicate special grace. To achieve this latter receptivity to "rational feeling" or affective knowing, Edwards occasionally applies figurative language, about which he is as skeptical as is Locke, in a way that cancels meanings based on natural reason and the natural world. Specifically, on these occasions Edwards undermines the conventional associations attached to certain words, and sometimes even the analogical performance of words. He apparently designs these procedures to make his audience *sense* a fundamental instability not only in their assumption of the reliability of language but also in their assumption of the reliable referentiality of reason and nature, the source of language. By thus undercutting what he perceives in his audience to be a prideful sense of security based on reason, nature, and language—only reflections of the images and shadows of the empirical world (idealistically assessed)—Edwards seeks to bring the prospective saint to the brink of an intuitive affective perception that Edwards cannot himself name. Edwards cannot cross the threshold between *sciential* and *sapiential* knowledge any more than John Bunyan can take Christian and the reader, at the end of *Pilgrim's Progress* (1678), across the threshold separating the nameable miseries of earthly existence and the ineffable wonders of heavenly existence.

From Something to Nothing to Everything
Edwards's Early Sermons

Sometime in the early or middle 1730s, Edwards delivered "Pressing into the Kingdom of God," a sermonic version of Bunyan's narrative that explicitly exhorts its audience to abandon a false sense of security in material reality and in the exercises of the self; it also implicitly communicates this message through the destabilizing of its audience's associations pertaining to the images of doors and gates. Edwards cites several scriptural references to gates, the most critical of which is Jesus' invitation to the elect: "Enter ye in at the strait gate: for wide is the gate and broad is the way that leadeth to destruction," whereas "strait is the gate, and narrow is the way that leadeth unto life, and few there be that find it" (Matthew 8:13-14). Of the scriptural references to doors, perhaps the most important in this sermon is the instance in Revelation (3:20): "Behold, I stand at the door, and knock: if any man hear my voice, and open the door, I will come in to him."

On first encounter, both of these passages appear to encourage a hopeful disposition in their hearer. The passage from Matthew, like the one from Revelation, might be interpreted as a generous invitation that implies the possibility of efficacious human action. Of course, in conservative Puritan theology each person was instructed to act, but at the same time admonished not to conclude that one's action could achieve anything of a redemptive nature or would necessarily signify one's final spiritual disposition. In that theology, justification precedes sanctification, and every human action serves as an opportunity which the deity might make use of or might reject at will. In these terms, the two scriptural passages from Matthew and Revelation, on second thought, may be interpreted from a perspective contrary to the first impression we noted. These passages imply an invitation, but they also suggest that the gateway or doorway is narrow and inaccessible to most and that the threshold is transversed only if Christ decides to initiate the inviting knock.

Edwards exploits this ambiguity of signification in his management of the images of the gate and the door as logogic sites in "Pressing into the Kingdom of God." Pertinently, near the very end of the sermon he says, "behold the door that God opens for you,"[33] and unlike the scriptural invitation to behold Christ at the door of the human heart, Edwards means for his audience, who inherently cannot comprehend the wonder of Christ, to indeed behold the *door*. The door is a signifier, an image or shadow of divine meaning. It is a logogic vehicle that, like John the Baptist as described by Edwards at the opening of the sermon, is a "forerunner" and an "instrument" of divine meaning; it is, like all sermonic language, an example of how "God influences persons by means."

But just as Edwards reports that John the Baptist said of Jesus and himself, "He must increase, but I must decrease," so too the logogic site must not become a symbol of iconic idolatry, something the hearer might seize upon in his or her desire for comforting security. On the contrary, to avoid this human tendency to find ways of appropriating meanings that encourage "liv[ing] a secure and careless life," Edwards exploits the scriptural ambiguity behind the images of the gateway and the doorway by making them at once seem comforting and threatening, until at the sermon's end he has destabilized associations attached to these images by shaking the foundations of their conventional signification. It is with irony, albeit rightfully instructive irony from Edwards's viewpoint, that at the end of his sermon he exhorts his audience to "behold the door."

Throughout the sermon doors and gates are associated with

safety. The gateway to a town represents an exit from the "snares" of the "wilderness," Edwards explains, not only literally in Northampton but figuratively as a passage to the kingdom of God from the earthly existence where "the state of the nation, and of this land, never looked so threatening of . . . [calamity] as at this day." So too with the portal of the home, behind the locked doors of which one may presumably find safety and security from something "pursuing you behind" while you are "groping in darkness." Outside the town gate, as outside the home portal, "one moment's delay is dangerous; for wrath is pursuing and divine vengeance hanging over every uncovered person."

In these contexts, the doorway and the gateway would appeal to Edwards's audience as icons of security, testaments to the human ability to build these features and thereby to be efficacious in managing its own escape from danger. This implication of self-reliance would appeal to their increasing eighteenth-century appreciation of self-determination, an appreciation reflected (for Edwards) in their reliance on the ability of words like "gate" and "door" to signify fixed comforting meanings, similar perhaps to their reaction to the two passages from Matthew and Revelation. But Edwards wishes to assail the person who is "in a great measure satisfied and quieted with his own works and performances," who derives a sense of control through such metonymic actions as passing through gates and doors. And so in "Pressing into the Kingdom of God" Edwards finally carefully destroys the icons of these two images in an effort to level his audience's self-reliance.

He manages this effect principally by suggesting that doorways and gateways are not as predictable as his audience believes, that the performance and signification of such thresholds should not be taken for granted because they are not finally under human control at all. In short, gates and doors may not open when we most need them to, or they may open when we most do not want them to. So we may find that we "stand at the door and knock, and cry, Lord, Lord, open to us, in vain"; or we may find that we are caught sitting still, or securely asleep, or with slack hands when Christ apocalyptically thrusts open the door. When Christ "knocks at many persons' doors, and at your door among the rest," we may find an invitation to cross the threshold of life into heaven or we may find an indictment sentencing us to hell. If we answer that divine knock, we might be saved; if we do not answer it, we might be damned (the odds are small that God would provide us with a deathbed conversion); yet, if we do answer it, we might find ourselves condemned anyway. One thing is certain: the doorway or gateway is utterly out of our control. Christ determines how it will function, just as he determines the fate of those who must eventually pass through it. Christ's knock may result in an invitation to leave the false security of our earthly home for the real security of the heavenly abode, or, should we ignore it, it may result in the unstoppable incursion of divine wrath right into our homes and hearts. This knock at the door, as Edward Taylor noted in 1690, may not necessarily "secure mee from," but may possibly "knock me down to, woe" (1.39, line 24).

Edwards's sermon appropriately stresses the potential benignity of the knock at the door of the homelike heart, but he readily equivocates, even at the end of the sermon, in order to keep discomforting ambiguity at large. He thus hedges: "it is *probable* some who are now awakened, will never obtain salvation"; "now there *seems* to be a door opened for old sinners"; and "there is the greatest *probability* that you will succeed" (emphasis added). We are left at the end of the sermon with the ambiguous "behold the door." Is the knock at the door an invitation or a threat? Just as in life one cannot know whether the Christ who will pass through that doorway will be a friend or a foe, so too, in Edwards's view, the passageway of words (as constructs of nature and *sciential* reason) always conceal, more than reveal, divine definitions. The best that words can do, therefore, is (like any doorway or gateway) to hint at this Christic eschatological definition through a form of dialogic contrariness that tends to erase any firm sense of connotative associations. For Edwards, such words as *gate*, *door*, and *knock* are ambiguous logogic sites that at best serve as signifying precursory instruments, like John the Baptist. Without the ideal meaning underlying them, they are nothing at all, and like John the Baptist, they should not be regarded as icons of security-promoting fixed meaning. On the contrary, they should be treated merely as pointers, unstable signifiers that must necessarily decrease in their promise to signify as the "light" of a *sapiential* appreciation of the divine excellence (which no words can truly signify) increases in the saint's mind.

By appropriating the ambiguity of the scriptural passages we noted concerning the gate and the door, Edwards apparently seeks to adumbrate, at the logogic sites in his sermon, the nature of the Second Coming of the Logos: "he shakes all their old foundations, and rouses them out of their resting places; so that they cannot quiet themselves with those things that formerly kept them secure." This comment describes precisely Edwards's erosion of the foundations of reliable meaning at his logogic sites, an erasure designed to "uncover" (to use his word) the security of the self (heart/home) based on certain rational interpretations and expectations that prove to be as shadowy as is (in Edwards's opinion) the material world itself. In "uncovering" an abiding ambiguity at the logogic site, the instability of secure verbal meaning even in seemingly fixed biblical passages like the ones referring to the gate and the door, Edwards potentially serves as a John-the-Baptist figure who here prophesies the possible Christic "uncovering" of, or Christic opening of the door to, his hearer's self.

Edwards's management of the words *door*, *gate*, and *knock* in "Pressing into the Kingdom of God" shares a number of similarities with the use of logogic cruxes by his predecessors, principally when these sites become places for the intersection of opposing meanings. But he differs from his predecessors, at least the ones reviewed in the foregoing chapters, by a more negative sense of the logogic crux. As the quotation from John the Baptist indicates, Edwards felt that material prophetic words should themselves dissolve before the idealism of divine definition. For Edwards, the role of rational language as an instrument of meaning should steadily decrease in value for the saint, who has crossed the threshold of the knocked-on door of the heart (self) and now experiences an ever-increasing Christic *sapiential* illumination beyond the capacity of language to convey genuinely in the slightest way.

"The True Christian's Life, a Journey Towards Heaven" (sometimes titled "The Christian Pilgrim"), another sermon written in the 1730s and mentioned earlier in passing, reveals Edwards's employment of a traditional Puritan image of what exists behind the door of one's house. In this sermon the radical logogic site of the family, so central to Ward and Oakes, is vexed. Initially in this sermon Edwards resorts to the archetypal Puritan image of the family in order to stimulate the collective memory of his audience. In this way, Edwards seeks to elicit in his audience a sense of security identified with such a familiar image, and then he counters this very reaction.[34]

In the second pararaph of this sermon, Edwards relates this image to the secure biblical context of "Abraham and Sarah, and their kindred," the first family of the chosen people of God. The implication of the stability of generations of blessed families—"all my fathers"—that this biblical context intimates is reinforced rhetorically a few paragraphs later: "If we are surrounded with many outward enjoyments, and things that are very comfortable to us; if we are settled in families, and have those good friends and relations that are very desirable; if we have companions whose society is delightful to us; if we have children that are pleasant and hopeful, and in whom we see many promising qualifications; if we live by good neighbors; have much of the respect for others; have a good name; are generally beloved where we are known; and have comfortable and pleasant accommodations; yet we ought not to take our rest in these things." The parallelism of this sentence is accretive, developing a tensile strength and density that rhetorically mimic the nature of material reality, as perceived by humanity, as if that material reality were something firmly solid and real. The rhetorical turn at the end of this incremental sequence—"yet we ought not"—comprises a reversal, but this counterpoint is not sufficient to "outweigh" the "natural force" of the preceding rhetorical sequence.

In characteristic fashion, Edwards reserves the key reversal for later in his sermon when he iconoclastically assails the image of the family, despite its biblically sanctioned implication of secure proliferation of generations in time. First, he encourages his audience to relate comfortably to the biblical and traditional image of family generation. Then, to counter what he perceives as his parishioners' engagement in "secular business, or . . . the care of a family" as an end in itself, he smashes the verbal icon as a sign, even as "Death will blow up" all of our "expectations" of "significancy." Edwards believes that the image of the family has become for his parishioners a Bablic monument of self-worship, merely one more reflector of "the vanity of this world."

At an important point he applies analogies, usually the building of blocks of *sciential* knowing that lead to a sense of increased security concerning stable meanings in the world. In this instance, however, Edwards's analogies suggest insubstantiality, instability, scattering, and dissolution; these analogies comprise a form of rhetorical dying that "blows up" the verbal icon of the family: "fathers and mothers, husbands, wives, or children, or the company of any, or all earthly friends . . . are but shadows; but the enjoyment of God is the substance. These are but scattered beams; but God is the sun. These are but streams; but God is the fountain. These are but drops; but God is the ocean." This impermanence of the family is fundamentally exposed by death, which takes away "those who were so dear to us," such as parents "taken away from their dear children." If the image of the family often serves as a reflector of human prideful idolatry, its destroyer, "the death of others," indeed provides a true "glass" (mirror) in which one "can see the vanity of this world" and in which one can discover why humanity should possess a heart "loose from these things" of the insubstantial material world.

Since the family is revealed by death to be insubstantial, the temporal world, for which the family is a metonymy, is revealed by mortality to be unreliable. Fundamentally, the temporal world provides no natural or verbal signs—such as the *image* or icon of the family—of secure substantial meanings. The connotative meanings of these signs are as mortal as are the humans reading them. To expose the void at the core of the secular idolization of such temporal signs, Edwards blows up (to use his words) the verbal icon of the image of the family in "The True Christian's Life." Presumably, bereft of the comfort of this image, Edwards's audience might henceforth commence the task of the Christian pilgrim: to journey toward his or her future "everlasting abode," where he or she may discover the denotative divine definition that has been occluded by the distracting secular and temporal connotations evident in humanity's self-idolization in such iconic signs as the family.

Whereas Edwards's predecessors, Ward and Oakes (chapter 3), artistically managed the traditional image of the family as a wondrous logogic site where material and divine meanings intertwine, Edwards is wary of it, at least during the 1730s. Given his sense of how much his parishioners have extracted secular self-definition from the image of the family, he approaches this logogic crux in "The True Christian's Life" as an icon of self-idolatry. In his iconoclastic response to this image in this sermon, Edwards does not quite undercut the rhetorical function of analogy itself, even though he does not use analogy to reinforce *sciential* "expectations" of "significancy." On this occasion, his analogies resist this expectation by undermining the traditional image of the family in order to expose it as a possible reflector (glass, mirror) of human vanity seeking "support" in the images and shadows of the insubstantial secular world.

Edwards's central image of the journey in this sermon is another traditional analogy, one that escapes the iconoclastic hammering evident in his treatment of the image of the family. However, even the analogized journey introduces a note of insecurity, for Edwards suggests in this sermon, as he did in "Pressing into the Kingdom of God," that one's arrival at "home" does not necessarily result in a curtailment of the perils one encountered while abroad. Heaven or hell, "one or the other of these must be our journey's end," Edwards explains, and "the bulk of mankind" arrives at hell.

A still more radical use of analogy occurs in "The Excellency of Christ," another early sermon by Edwards. The central thesis of this work argues that Christ represents the conjunction of completely antithetical qualities, such as his theanthropic joining of divine wrath and divine mercy, and of infinite sublimity and infinite degradation. At the outset Edwards warns his audience that the "conjunction of such excellencies in Christ" is beyond the human "manner of conceiving."[35] This wonder is essentially a paradox that is not accessible to *sciential* modes of reasoning. But Edwards knows that, despite this warning, his audience will rely on the capacity of words to convey this mystery to them at a rational level. He anticipates that his audience will think they are being reverently attentive in this expectation. He suspects that they are unaware of the self-idolatrous pride this very expectation reveals. So he manages a logogic site early in "The Excellency of Christ" to expose this prideful reliance on their ability to use their limited reason to derive some comfort from language about this mystery.

The imagery of this early passage is authorized by Isaiah 40:15, which Edwards exploits in an effort to make his audience understand the paradoxical nature of Christ not through *sciential* reasoning but through an affective knowing suggestive of *sapiential* reasoning. The passage reads: "Christ, as he is God, is infinitely great and high above all. He is higher than the kings of the earth: for he is King of kings and Lord of lords. He is higher than the heavens, and higher than the highest angels of heaven. So great is he, that all men, all kings and princes, are as worms of the dust before him; all nations are as the drop of the bucket, and the light dust of the balance; yea, and angels themselves are as nothing before him. He is so high, that he is infinitely . . . above our conceptions, that we cannot comprehend him." The images, basically analogies, in this passage serve collectively as a logogic site where Edwards reveals their concealment of divine truth.

Note, first, Edwards's initial chain of imagery in this passage. He indicates that Christ is higher (more exalted) than kings, then higher than the heavens, then higher than the angels. The sequence of these images forms a pattern of ascent, and this pattern represents an "ascending" rational expectation in the audience, as if the human mind could use words as a

Tower of Babel to ascend defiantly toward a rational comprehension of the divine realm. In mapping (and initially encouraging) this rational expectation Edwards exposes his audience's prideful sense of security in the capacity of the human mind to reason (particularly through language) toward a closure with divine truth. This revelation becomes evident in the next movement of his imagery.

If anyone in Edwards's audience was enticed rationally to anticipate hearing something about God—the reasonable expectation of the sequence from kings, heavens, and angels—he or she was disappointed. The tease of Edwards's transitional "So great is he" does not lead to some explicit revelation about God—the mind's desire for rational mastery; rather, it leads merely to a reiteration of the very same sequence, as if the first towerlike Bablic ascent of words had been dashed to the ground and had to be reconstructed again. This time the audience is directed in a chain of ascent from kings and princes, to nations, to angels.

But this second chain is actually an altered version of the first. This time, perhaps, it promises to be more successful than the first chain, in reaching divine meaning, by the application of analogies. Analogies are a crucial device in the operations of *sciential* thought, for which they serve as ladders of access connecting the unknown to the already known. Through analogy reason seems to conquer the unknown, and the towerlike ladder of analogy in this instance suggests that God, the incomprehensible, might be knowable by means of analogies based on the material world, which is all *scientia* can ever know.

But the analogies Edwards provides do not fulfill this rational expectation, any more than do the oxymorons of Bunyan's "Apology" in *Pilgrim's Progress*. On the contrary, they frustrate it; for the image of kings is likened to worms, the image of nations to drops and dust, and the image of angels to nothing. These analogies also form a pattern, one of descent from something (worms) to nothing. Instead of aiding the pattern of ascent comprised of the kings/nations/angels images, the analogical chain of descent comprised of worms/dust/

nothing creates a paradox in the rational mind, a paradox apropos Christ's nature as set forth in the sermon. This paradox amounts to a destruction of words, a smashing of their capacity into dust, to expose how they can, in their own nature, reveal *nothing* about divinity.

But if Edwards smashed words as verbal icons (as a form of human self-idolatry) to expose a void at their center (as at the center of the images and shadows of the natural forms on which they are based), this process potentially created as well a void in the mind of his early eighteenth-century hearer or reader, who presumably had also experienced the dashing of rational expectations (the work of *scientia* vis-a-vis language and nature). In one sense, Edwards had merely provided another instance of his argument: "you have been seeking something, but yet remain destitute." Confronted with this void—the blanking of the rational mind before the paradox of antithetical ascending and descending imagery—the human mind might paradoxically experience a preliminary affective awareness of the paradoxical nature of Christ. In supplanting natural reason with an intimation of this affective reason, Edwards conveyed a preliminary impression of a higher mode of knowing: *sapiential* perception, which special grace progressively restores to the human self (now humbly empty of self-idolatry through natural signs, now reduced to "nothing").

The management of language in these three sermons is similarly evident in "The Justice of God in the Damnation of Sinners," a sermon delivered in the 1730s that may serve as a fitting final example of Edwards's treatment of the logogic crux. Like "The Excellency of Christ," this sermon briefly mentions that Christ "is infinitely exalted above the greatest potentates of the earth, and the highest angels in heaven,"[36] but the imagery of this biblical allusion does not serve as an occasion for the breaking of verbal icons. In this sermon, that occasion is provided by "what things soever the law saith, it saith to them who are under the law: that every month may be stopped, and all the world may become guilty before God" and, even more precisely, that "their throat is an open sepulchre; with their tongues they have used deceit" (Romans 3:13, 19). In "The

Justice of God in the Damnation of Sinners" the image of the mouth speaking language becomes itself a logogic site *par excellence*.

Throughout this sermon Edwards details various misuses of speech, especially as expressed in blaspheming, quarreling, idle talking, licentious singing, lying, and an uncharitable condemning of others. People are so engaged in their boisterous self-gratifying (perverse) uses of language, Edwards indicates, that they cannot hear the Word of God: Christ's calls, councils, warnings, commands. Moreover, even among those who think they have heard that Word, their mouths are not stopped; for many of them Edwards observes, open their mouths to boast their righteousness, on the one hand, or to excuse themselves from the execution of justice, on the other hand. And even if some of these people have not made either claim in spoken language, they have done so in the language of thought; they have not really heard "the mouth of conscience" and not "been quiet in the frame of [their] mind," where they have deceived themselves about their boasts or excuses.

Edwards's assault on language, as spoken or as thought, his exposure of how (in Pauline terms) the human tongue is used in external and internal deceit, is conveyed in this sermon in at least two dramatic moments. The first occurs very early in the work when Edwards includes the point of view of his audience in a manner that indicts them through the very nature of their everyday mode of discourse. "Our obligations to love, honor, and obey any being, is in proportion to his loveliness, honor, and authority; for that is the very meaning of the *words*. When we *say* any one is very lovely, it is the same as to *say*, that he is one very much to be loved: or if we *say* such a one is more honorable than another, the meaning of the *words* is, that he is one that we are more obliged to honor. If we *say* any one has great authority over us, it is the same as to *say*, that he has great right to our subjection and obedience" (emphasis added). We say these things, and they are true denotatively, Edwards indicates; yet we deceive ourselves in their iteration. For "common sense" (Edwards's appropriation of that favorite expression of the eighteenth century) indicates that God "is infinitely lovely," "infinitely more honorable than they," and "infinitely worthy to be obeyed"; and common sense indicates that any violation of these "infinite obligations" requires "infinite punishment." Yet we completely deceive ourselves with the very words of truth we speak aloud or in our minds. And in terms of this deception, our words become a self-indictment, making our mouths open sepulchres, emblems of our merited eternal death.

A second and even more dramatic moment occurs a little past midway in the sermon when Edwards anticipates the interior language of his audience and speaks it aloud. "I am sensible that by this time many persons are ready to *open their mouths* in objection against this. If all should *speak* what they now think, we should hear *murmuring* all over the meetinghouse, and one and another would *say,* 'I cannot see how this can be, that I be not willing that Christ should be my Saviour, when I would give all the world that he was my Saviour'" (emphasis added). Again Edwards demonstrates not only that their mouths are not stopped—clearly (in the context of the sermon) a sign of the unregenerate—but also that their words in this and other instances comprise a form of their self-deception. He indicates the impurity of the motives informing their words, a "devoutness" that amounts to "mere dissembling." Simply put, their desire to "escape from misery" (eternal damnation) disguises a "forced compliance" in the image of a "free willingness" to follow Christ, whose infinite excellencies (loveliness, honor, and authority) do not *intrinsically* inform the motives of Edwards's audience. Concerning these Christic excellencies, "your heart does not go out after Christ, of itself."

Of course, the heart, as finite, cannot close with Christ, the infinite; and if that heart were justified and sanctified by saving grace (conveying an affective sense of the infinite), its physical and mental mouth would indeed be stopped before the wonder of these divine excellencies. It is a matter of *sense.* Common sense, as Edwards indicates, can lead us to a recognition of the gap between the finite and the infinite, but only a gracious sense, an affective rationality, can convey an intimation of the wonder of divinity. As Edwards bluntly tells his audience, "You never had a sight or sense of any such excellency or worthiness in Christ." As a result, the common sense informing their spoken or thought arguments is denotatively senseless. Merely "saying it is so . . . is a very different thing from . . . any spiritual sight or sense of Christ's excellency."

This spiritual sense, an affective rationality, defies the capacity of language, rooted in nature and natural reason. This gracious sense urges a stopped mouth, the eschatological end of language in the soul that adumbrates the fulfillment of the Logos at the end of time (the Second Coming). Then, as ideally now, the saint's mouth would be stopped in wonder and awe. As Edwards indicates in "The Excellency of Christ," no language of the mouth or mind can possibly close with the infinite excellencies of the deity. And as he similarly indicates in "The Justice of God in the Damnation of Sinners," language is in fact a fallen medium based on nature and natural reason that is the principal deceiving component of one's faulty self-definition. Language must be used to praise God in prayer and sermons, but at the end of time even these corrupt modes must vanish.

Edwards does not seek to mediate between muteness and voice, as did Bradstreet and Taylor (chapter 2), whose attitude seems to anticipate an apocalyptic fulfillment or replenishment of the polysemous wonder of nature and language. In contrast, Edwards leaves his audience with a potentially terrifying impression of the impossibility of either using language in a regenerate manner or of ceasing to use language at all. He prophesies a complete regenerative emptying of the self, a complete eschatological erasure of language and the consciousness it informs as sources of any genuine sense of self.

Hence the closing words of "The Justice of God in the Damnation of Sinners" are prefaced with an apt quotation from Ezekiel (16:63): "That thou mayest remember and be confounded, and never open thy mouth any more, because of thy shame." Edwards follows this quotation with a paradoxical statement that presumably is designed to stymie spoken or thought words, even as did his destruction of analogical patterns in "The Excellency of Christ." "You should never open your mouth in boasting, or self-justification," he indicates in his final sentence in the sermon, "but you have reason . . . to open your mouth in God's praises . . . for his rich, unspeakable, and sovereign mercy to you." In short, one's physical and mental mouth should be stopped, but since that act is impossible for the human self, then one should fill that open sepulchre of the mouth with words of praise; but these words of praise themselves are empty because they are utterly inadequate to articulate the "unspeakable" excellencies of the Redeemer. Edwards's passage moves from muteness, to connotative speech, to fundamental denotative muteness. In this paradoxical instruction, the final words of the sermon, Edwards reminds his audience of their fallen condition, emblemized in language itself, as well as of the eschatological muteness, in wonder and awe, of the true saint. For him silence is indeed golden.

As we have seen, in his early sermons Edwards approaches language as replete with icons of self-interest. Initially in these writings he encourages his audience to do what he thinks they already do far too often: to use their natural reason to develop a prideful sense of security based on rational expectations founded on the seemingly solid "images and shadows" of the material world. Then he undercuts these images in various ways in order to frustrate his audience's rational expectations and thereby to create a pride-reducing space or void or emptiness. By this means potentially experiencing an affective sense of the instability of *sciential* knowledge, Edwards's ideal hearer or reader barely glimpses from the verge of this void *(aporia)* a *sapiential* knowing, an intuitive wisdom based on pure idea rather than natural phenomena. This foreshadowed perception would become realized, as we learned from *A Divine and Supernatural Light*, were Christ to bestow special grace, which "assimilates the nature [of the soul] to the divine nature, and changes the soul into an image of the same glory that is beheld."

In effect, in his sermons of the 1730s Edwards approaches words, which he believes are based on nature, as idols, material signs that people turn into graven images in a religion of reason that derives from these mere shadows of the material world a false security concerning the meaning of reality and of life. Like early English Puritans in reaction to Anglican church art, especially during the English Civil War in the 1640s,[37] Edwards in effect smashes icons, verbal "graven images," "any likeness *of any thing* . . . that *is* in the earth" (Exodus 20:4). Edwards evokes Bradstreet's and Taylor's anxious management of the verbal icon as a logogic site, particularly how their mutual destruction of the surface structure of their poetic monuments recalls this second commandment, as rephrased in Leviticus 26:1: "Ye shall make you no idols nor graven image, neither rear you up a standing image, neither shall ye set up *any* image of stone in your land, to bow down unto it" (cf. Psalms 97:7). However, whereas Bradstreet, Taylor, Richard Mather, Ward, and Oakes could coalesce both this biblical restriction and the counterbalancing Augustinian tradition of the word as authorized by the Incarnate Word, Edwards polarizes sharply toward the iconoclastic impulse of his predecessors. He exploits the logogic site not to reveal the manifold entwining of the eternal and the material, simultaneously suggesting hope and despair; on the contrary, he treats the logogic crux as a Trojan horse to be broken open to reveal the concealed emptiness at the core of all material manifestations (images and shadows), including human language (based on nature and natural reason). This void at the center of human language intimates the presence of a divine reality that cannot be said or named in *sciential* discourse but that can be affectively registered as "mental sensation."

This approach to the logogic site is not the result of Edwards's deaccentuation of the Incarnation in his theology but of his response to the times, as he assessed them. As he saw the early eighteenth century, too many people were trusting to reason (really limited *sciential* reasoning, he thought) and to natural laws as indices to the meaning of life, a trust expressed (he thought) in their attitude of security concerning the meaning of words and nature. For Edwards, denotation really lies only in pure idea, something the *sciential* capacity of the mind cannot know because of its utter dependence upon representational, connotative signs. So in his early sermons he at first

Breaking Verbal Icons 119

teased his audience to respond to the verbal icon as if it were indeed the "something" they thought it was in the course of their daily activity. Then he shattered this same verbal icon in order to rupture the rational expectations of his audience to elicit in them a new sense of "nothing." This sense of a proper humility, an emptiness of any rational security (pride, self-interest, self-idolatry), is requisite to a true knowledge of divine reality ("everything"), the denotative idea that is only inadequately intimated by the confusing, shadowy connotative signs of the natural world. In terms of Edwards's theological idealism, the denotative reality of God can only be encountered as *sapiential* pure idea (affective knowledge initiated by special grace) because God's excellence is incomprehensible and therefore unimagable, unrepresentable, and unaccountable in terms of *sciential* reason and its language, both of which remain utterly dependent on Bablic natural and verbal connotative signs.

5

Islands of Meaning

As our initial review of Renaissance and Reformed perspectives on writing indicates, the Puritan dual attitude toward the ambiguity of human language—at once a problem and an opportunity—had a long history. In the preceding chapters I have tried to explore one aesthetic feature of the Puritans' profound exploitation of this binary nature of language. Specifically, in their exuberant and nervous artistry, Puritan authors often hesitated at an ambiguous logogic site to contemplate the intertwining of the divine and the human in postlapsarian verbal expression. No firm case can be made that this Puritan emphasis on logogic cruxes of equivocal meanings had a direct or special influence on the artistic management of language by their successors. But it is interesting, if only as a curiosity perhaps, to observe two instances of later American writings, one representing the end of the eighteenth century and one representing the end of the nineteenth century. These two works may be imaginatively included in this study of *Puritan* American literature insofar as they specifically draw upon their Puritan heritage and primarily function (whether by authorial intent or not) in terms of logogic cruxes similar to those scrutinized by early colonial Puritans.

However, if these two later documents seem to articulate with this Puritan heritage, their attitude toward the logogic site differs from that of their predecessors. In contrast to the seventeenth-century Puritan writings we have discussed, these two works do not affirm that a transparent denotative mean-

Islands of Meaning 121

ing—however dispersed or obscure or remote as a referent—may potentially be concealed within the temporal vying connotations of words. In these two works the equivocal logogic crux does not humble the author and the reader before the mystery of divine revelation obscurely intertwined with "the mutable things of this unstable world," but jolts their audience with the puzzling nature of language itself. They both suggest that something is indeed concealed in language, as if it were a Trojan horse; however, principally they both suggest that language conceals its own inadequacy to impart anything ultimately denotative. The text from the end of the eighteenth century plays with this issue by problematically intertwining humor and polemic into a religiopolitical Gordian knot. The text from the end of the nineteenth century similarly fuses a utopian political message with a paradoxical critique of the capacity of language to reveal anything more than its own hidden inefficacy.

Eighteenth-Century Allegory or Satire?
Nathan Fiske's "An Allegorical Description"

In April 1790, *The Massachusetts Magazine* (pp. 228-30) published a short work of prose entitled "An Allegorical Description of a Certain Island and Its Inhabitants," which it presented as the sixteenth entry for a column designated as "The Philanthropist." This brief allegory is a curious document. It has been interpreted as an early example of American utopian literature celebrating humanity's eventual reunion with God in heaven, the true utopia.[1] However, a reconsideration of this work is in order because its ostensible rational religious message is vexed and subverted by the preponderance of emotionally charged political terms pervading the essay. Although American revolutionary and post-revolutionary rhetoric sometimes evidences a successful integration of religious and political discourse,[2] such a harmonious coalescence does not occur in this particular work, whatever its author may have intended. When the political features of "An Allegorical Description" are scrutinized in relation to the sentiments of its prospective patriotic early national proletarian audience, the meaning of this writing becomes so problematic that the reader is left with questions about the reliability of the narrator, the intent of the author, and the nature of language.

"An Allegorical Description" tells a simple story. On an "imprisoning isle," a place of broken shores and surfaces as well as "tempestuous winds," some "sort of exiles" serve their sentence and "do penance." Bearing "marks of degradation and disgrace," these "people, by some misdemeanor, have, at some time or other, incurred the displeasure of their sovereign." But they will not remain "in a state of perpetual banishment, unless they continue incorrigibly rebellious." Many of these exiles believe that they will be permitted to "return" to their "native country" if during their sentence on the island "they manifest a strict allegiance to their sovereign."

Even the terms of this plot summary convey political overtones. Such words as *exiles, sovereign, rebellious, banishment, allegiance,* and *native country* doubtless elicited political memories for the American reader of 1790. And these words are readily reinforced in the allegory by the following expressions: "their king," "this monarch," "absolute prince," "royal orders," "summons of their prince," "faulty subjects," and "this colony." Moreover, some say the "King of *Utopia*" is "amiable" and "benevolent," whereas others describe him as "arbitrary," "inexorable," and "tyrannical." The terms of this debate would have recalled for some American readers the difference between fire-and-brimstone and affective Congregationalism; but these same terms also would have recalled for still more post-revolutionary readers discussions concerning King George during the war years.

Even the carefully selected opening and closing quotation from Edward Young's "The Christian Triumph," in *Night Thoughts* (1742-44), contains such political references as "This dark, incarcerating *Colony*," "breaks their chain," "manumits," and "calls . . . [the] exile home." The placement of this quotation from Young at the start and the end of the article would indeed seem to cue the reader to read the allegory in religious terms,[3] specifically of the kind characteristic of the Puritan heritage of the regional readers of the *Massachusetts Magazine.* But the particular passage selected from Young's poem emphasizes words to which eighteenth-century Americans had been highly sensitized by the recent political upheaval of the new nation. The total effect of these logogic cruxes vies with any orthodox religious reading of the allegory. For if the religious message of the text seems to argue for complete "submission to God's will,"[4] the political message evidently does not. In fact, extremely few conventional terms drawn from religious discourse actually occur in the narrative. The apparent religious message is virtually embedded in cant derived from recent American political rhetoric. In invoking the recent revolt against a slavelike submission to the king of England, the political language of "An Allegorical Description" seems to satirize subservience, especially since priestlike or ministerlike "monitors, who are also interpreters of the royal orders, agree not among themselves" and since the islanders personally possess the power to make "their exile agreeable or painful." At the level of political nuance, the allegory seems to urge the reader to make the best of banishment by the king, which is of course what Americans did when they chose independence and declared their country, in Thomas Paine's words, ready to "receive the fugitive" and to serve as "an asylum for mankind."[5]

In short, the emotionally charged political language of the allegory subverts its ostensible rational religious message. These two connotative levels of meaning fuse together and resist the reader's urge—the urge elicited by earlier Puritan logogic cruxes—to decode certainly its intimated underlying or concealed denotative revelation. As a religious parable, "An Allegorical Description" is a fiasco. Whatever its author's intention, this work also reads as a political satire on religion and, accordingly, subverts the apparent religious message by implicitly suggesting that its American audience should liberate itself from too submissive a faith in a divine King even as it has emancipated itself from a debilitating faith in an earthly king.

To identify the emotional appeal to the post-revolutionary American reader of this undermining political language, in which the religious message of the allegory is essentially enmeshed, it is helpful to contextualize the appearance of "An Allegorical Description" in *The Massachusetts Magazine*. This magazine, which lasted for eight years (1789-1796), was one of the foremost[6] and was the longest lived[7] of the eighteenth-century American periodicals. It was initially edited by Isaiah Thomas (1749-1831), the most important publisher in his time.[8] Thomas inherited a commercial rather than a religious heritage, and there is evidence that in the 1780s he published the first American edition of the lascivious *Memoirs of a Woman of Pleasure* by John Cleland.[9]

In *The Massachusetts Magazine*, however, he prudently declared that his periodical would print nothing "incompatible with pure morality, nor adverse to the grand principles of religion" (1 [December 1789],1). This statement did not mean that his publication would be concerned primarily with matters of religion, but rather "the grand cause of Religion, Virtue, Reason" (5 [January 1793], iv). This ready integration of religious belief and reason was (as we saw in chapter 4) precisely the target of Jonathan Edwards forty years earlier. It was now typical of the thought of many of Thomas's contemporaries,[10] and it prepares the reader for what he indeed did publish in his magazine: works, like "An Allegorical Description," that were secularly moral and entertaining in a way that would be compatible with the grand principles of a very *generalized* religious belief. For example, in possibly intimating the renunciation of passive submission to the divine King and the need for humanity to make the best of exile through its own effort, "An Allegorical Description" is generally Deistic. It potentially indicates that "none are ignorant to whose jurisdiction they belong," yet "all have reasonable grounds to believe, that if they will but accommodate their minds to their situation, it will be comfortable."

Deistic sentiment as such was probably not intended by Nathan Fiske, whose posthumously published, two-volume *The Moral Monitor* (1801) included "An Allegorical Descrip-

Islands of Meaning 125

tion" among other essays on various subjects. Fiske was a Congregationalist minister in Brookfield, Massachusetts. Although he never advocated a radical populism and in fact warned against the influence of Paine (*A Sermon Preached at the Dudleian Lecture*, 1796), Fiske was decidedly liberal in his views and a strong ally of the patriot gentry during the revolutionary period. Particularly evident in "An Allegorical Description" is Fiske's well-known enthusiasm, which he shared with Deists, for self-improvement and the public good. In 1792, he was awarded an honorary doctorate by Harvard for his efforts on behalf of Christian love and tolerance.

Thomas, too, apparently emphasized tolerance in shaping his magazine to attract a wide readership, and he possibly found Fiske's essay particularly congenial to his editorial goals. Thomas aimed, in his own words, "to compile a periodical not only for those whose cultural advantages had been considerable, but for a proletarian class which, until now, had neither supported nor found reason for supporting magazines" (1 [December 1789], 1). The background of this class—Thomas's declared audience—provides an especially good clue to the political nuance many late eighteenth-century American readers might have detected in "An Allegorical Description." This early national proletarian class was primarily composed of patriots. They were the commoners to whom Thomas Paine had pitched a number of his own writings during the revolutionary war, and they comprised the backbone of the democratic new republic. Isaiah Thomas was himself not only from this working class; he had himself been a patriot during the 1770s, when for his safety he had to flee from his home.

To the patriotic proletarian class of the 1790s, images of exile, denial of freedom, and arbitrary tyranny were commonplace, and they were principally expressed in the metaphor of enslavement.[11] The prevalence of this motif is apparent in such instances as Thomas Jefferson's emphasis on the words *liberty, freedom* and *independence* in his version of the Declaration of Independence; Jefferson's stress on resisting *submission* in "A Summary View of the Rights of British America";

George Washington's contrast between enslavement and freedom in his "Address to the Continental Army" in 1776; Thomas Paine's focus on servitude in *The Crisis*; and Philip Freneau's celebration of the end of bondage in "America Independent." Even in Letter IX of Hector St. John de Crèvecoeur's *Letters from an American Farmer* the metaphor of enslavement characterizes the relationship between the colonies and British justice.[12]

This imagery of submission, bondage, servitude, or enslavement signified the exercise of power and control by the arbitrary will of someone over the forced actions and the property of a subservient subject.[13] This imagery was used in eighteenth-century America not only to describe the general subservient state of the prewar colonies to British arbitrary power, but also to refer to the specific treatment of individuals at the hands of British representatives. Typically, even as early as 1724, Cotton Mather spoke of the treatment of the American colonists as a denial of "the Priviledges of Englishmen": "They had no more Priviledges left but This, that they were not Bought and Sold for Slaves."[14] Here, perhaps, Mather also hinted at the early Puritan settlers' sense of themselves as exiles in the new world, a condition intensified by the restoration of King Charles II.[15] Fifty years after Mather's comment, Jefferson not only specifically mentioned slavery in "A Summary View of the Rights of British America," but also spoke of the stationing of British armed forces in America in terms suggesting an incarceration or imprisonment. The metaphor of enslavement or near-enslavement (including the concept of imprisonment) applied not only to the specific behavior of British governmental appointees towards the American colonists, but also to the actual condition of exile in which very many of the post-revolutionary proletariat—the very people to whom Thomas explicitly addressed himself in the *Massachusetts Magazine*—had once found themselves.

Many of these people had been indentured workers who had purchased their passage to the New World with a bondagelike commitment for (usually) four years of future labor. Demographic evidence indicates that more than four-fifths of the

Islands of Meaning 127

prewar colonial artisans, even in the most highly skilled trades, were motivated to leave England because of economic need (including unemployment and the tyranny of landlords) and arrived on the American shore as indentured servants.[16] Dependent entirely on a labor market from which they could not derive any profit during their years of contracted servitude, many of these indentured workers spoke of their existence as a form of temporary exile, imprisonment, or slavery.[17]

If indentured workers as a class felt the weight of their interim bondage, the convicted criminals transported to America were downright irate about their exile, and with good reason. Whereas indentured servants could sometimes experience hardship and cruelty, transported fugitives were assured of both. There were over fifty thousand criminals shipped to America during the eighteenth century as a result of the Transportation Act of 1718. That resident colonists resented and heatedly denounced this imperial policy is abundantly evident, most notably in Benjamin Franklin's correspondence to *The Pennsylvania Gazette* in 1751 and *The London Chronicle* in 1759.[18] Like the indentured class, the convict class was driven by economic necessity, and their transport was equally a matter of enrichment for merchants. But unlike the indentured colonists, the transported criminals were minimally skilled in any trade, the supply of them to the colonies far outstripped demand, and more of them ran away.[19] Like the indentured workers, these convicts referred to their imprisonment as a form of "exile," "bondage," and "slavery," from which they too hoped to emerge into better economic prospects.[20] Although it was more difficult for them than for the indentured to blend into colonial society, after their term of sentence most of the transported fugitives in fact did not commit new criminal offenses and went on with their lives in the new world.[21]

The revolutionary war threw the transportation of convicts from Britain into chaos, and the British crown looked elsewhere for a place to send them. After years of complications and a horrible berth in anchored prison ships (cf. Philip Freneau's bitter *The British Prison Ship* recollecting a similar incarceration in New York), British fugitives were sent to a number of other locations, most notably Australia, an island very much like the one described in "An Allegorical Description." The first group of convicts landed in Australia in 1788, a tragic affair followed by efforts to deliver others in 1790.[22] Americans were aware of this new imperial decision, as is evident, for example, in Franklin's specific reference in 1787 to the shipment of felons to Botany Bay, Australia.[23] Would not the news of this new forced emigration make many Americans, not even ten years into their uncertain new republic, think in terms of the metaphor of servitude that had prevailed in prewar discourse on the imperial treatment of the colonies as well as on the imperial policy of transporting criminals to American shores? And would not the news of the harsh venture in Australia make many individual Americans personally recollect their previous servitude as indentured workers or convicts?

The export of criminals to Australia might well be one immediate target of "An Allegorical Description." This event would likely have offended Fiske's abiding principle of benevolence, even if he personally may not have identified with the working class. This event, moreover, would likely have interested Thomas, too. Although Thomas never experienced indenture or criminal conviction, he had been a laborer all of his adult life and, like his anticipated proletarian audience, he had been a patriot who protested the servitude of the colonies to the British. An allegorical work informed by the imagery of exile and submission that had prevailed in the prewar rhetoric of indentured servants, transported fugitives, and patriots had renewed commercial value in 1790, by which time the transport of British felons to Australia was known and doubtless evoked emotional memories among Thomas's prospective proletarian readership. The *prospective* proletarian class to whom Thomas appealed, we should recall, would have included by 1790 many patriots, some of the more than fifty thousand former transported convicts, and a significant number of American artisans, more than eighty per cent of whom had been indentured.

But if we can perhaps somewhat surmise Thomas's cogent sense of the economic viability of the appeal of revolutionary political rhetoric, playing off both the patriotism and the background of his prospective readership, we cannot even begin to speculate whether he recognized the degree to which the emotionally charged political language of Fiske's narrative potentially subverts the rational ostensible religious message of its allegory. Did Thomas even suspect that this narrative might be read as a political satire on religion related by an unreliable narrator who seems to suggest—doubtless far more tolerantly than Fiske intended—that all beliefs are merely a matter of perspective and that his American audience should liberate itself from too submissive a Calvinistic faith in a divine King even as it has emancipated itself from a debilitating Loyalist faith in an earthly king?

This question remains unanswered, one puzzle among several, about the enigmatical nature of Fiske's "An Allegorical Description of a Certain Island and Its Inhabitants." Its logogic cruxes evidence a playful interweaving of humor and polemic into a religiopolitical Gordian knot. Something is concealed within, as if it were a Trojan horse. But exactly what is hidden within this self-declared allegory? The reader of this document is left puzzling over the nature of language itself as a contemplative site of (permanently?) occluded denotative meaning. In one sense, among others, this connotative ambiguity might be interpreted as an expression of the numerous uncertainties of the early national period, akin to Bradford's perception a century and a half earlier of "the mutable things of this unstable world." Perhaps the logogic cruxes of this eighteenth-century document finally conceal only the inability of language to impart anything ultimately definitive, as if its words were like a colonial island similar to the one described in the account. Like that island, words in Fiske's text seem to evidence a Puritanlike religious heritage of firm meaning but now, like the new nation, also find themselves referentially unstable in their independence from the sovereign familial definitions of that heritage.

The Letter Killeth
Edward Bellamy's "To Whom This May Come"

Edward Bellamy's short story entitled "To Whom This May Come" (1889) is also a peculiar allegory about an island. Except for passing references to it in a very few of the studies of Bellamy's writings, it has attracted no attention. It is reprinted in facsimile in Arthur O. Lewis's *American Utopias*, but it receives almost no commentary in the editor's introduction.[24] In spite of this early and latter-day critical disregard, however, its appearance a year after the publication of *Looking Backward 2000-1887* (1888) and its inclusion as the last tale, as the last word, in *The Blindman's World and Other Stories* (1898) suggest that greater attention to this tale is warranted. The story evinces a curious intrinsic feature as well; for it is a work that paradoxically uses language to refute the cogency of language itself, a story that talks its way finally into a silence in which the ideal reader searches for an understanding that transcends the inability of words truly to communicate visionary ideational meaning.

"To Whom This May Come" is presented as a document written by a narrator who is shipwrecked on an island, where he encounters an advanced human race living in utopian conditions because this race has for centuries renounced language and developed telepathic visual communication. The narrator joins this happy society, even becoming romantically attached to one of its women. After the narrator learns to appreciate the advantages of life with these utopians, he experiences another disaster at sea that separates him from the islanders. Although rescued by a ship from his own civilization, he dies. Our world receives the narrator's document, recounting his encounter, through the agency of E.B., who confines himself to a mere single sentence appended as a note at the end of the narrative.

At first encounter the plot of this tale seems rather slight, and doubtless this fact to some degree accounts for the neglect of this story, even by Bellamy enthusiasts. But the plots of many nineteenth-century romances, typical stories by Nathaniel Hawthorne, for example, appear to be slight. The test of the artistic depth of nineteenth-century romance lies not in the complexity of its plot but rather in the complexity of its author's management of language—of nuance, allusion, and imagery among other logogic features. This is the level at which Bellamy's story needs to be investigated, all the more so because the story is so evidently about the nature of language.

My reference to Hawthorne is not gratuitous. While Bellamy served as a reviewer for the *Springfield Union* during the 1870s, he demonstrated a keen interest in the romance genre.[25] He knew the fiction of his predecessors and imitated it. Critics have, for instance, detailed Bellamy's indebtedness to Hawthorne in the fashioning of theme and character names, types, and behavior; this influence includes allegorical manner as well.[26] This issue of Hawthorne's influence, particularly in the practice of allegory, deserves further analysis; for "To Whom This May Come" reveals a use of allegory much more indebted to his and Hawthorne's mutual Puritan heritage, and much more profound and self-reflexive than Bellamy's critics have generally recognized in his writings.

Clues to the allegorical dimension of this story can be found in its many allusions to religious matter. These allusions are not surprising given the fact that Bellamy's father was a minister, that his family was of stern New England Calvinist heritage, that his early life was filled with religious preoccupations and reading, and that his break from this early experience resulted in a personal revision for Bellamy that blended New England religious tradition with a social evangelism. Christian concepts with a Puritan heritage informed Bellamy's development as a thinker,[27] but his essays in *The New Nation*, reprinted later as *Talks on Nationalism* (1938), make clear that for him the ideals of Christianity could finally be realized only in terms of the secular context of a material progress. In "To Whom This May Come" reference is made to "the virtue of confession for the soul," to "rending the veil of self," to "the false ego of the apparent self," among other similar passages.[28] Such expressions comprise the mainstay of religious discourse as much as they do a strand of an apparent theme in Hawthorne's writings, and they are applied by Bellamy to describe the nature of the utopian islanders, for whom mental telepathy has eliminated the barriers of disguised arrogant self-interest. Such expressions from routine religious discourse are reinforced by a reference to the utopians' belief in life after death and, more significantly, by a biblical allusion in the very last paragraph of the dying narrator's account, where he disparages "the stunning Babel of [his] nation of talkers" (pp. 414, 415).

This allusion to the Tower of Babel, appropriately situated in the final paragraph of the tale, is an important trace to Bellamy's allegorical message about the fallen nature of language, a meaning that unites the plot, the religious references, and the narrative manner of "To Whom This May Come." The account of the Tower of Babel, told in chapter 11 of Genesis, describes a time when the entire earth spoke one language. Some of Nimrod's people decided to build a miles-high tower, "whose top may reach unto heaven," but the deity was most displeased with this expression of egocentric pride (of the wrong kind of heavenly aspiration) and so "did there confound the language of all the earth" and "scatter them abroad upon the face of all the earth."

According to Christian tradition this tower was located in Babylon,[29] the archetypal city of corruption in New England theological discourse. Also according to Christian tradition the episode concerning the Tower of Babel (from the Hebrew *balal*, to confuse) is a replay of the fall of humanity. This connection to Adam and Eve after the Fall in Eden is in fact made in Bellamy's story when its narrator explains at one point that the ability of the utopians, who are "lords of themselves" (p. 411), to read his mind made him suddenly aware of his "nudity" (his word) and made him want "to run away and hide [him]self" (p. 397). This comment echoes a scriptural passage referring to Adam and Eve, who after eating the forbidden fruit suddenly "knew that they were naked," clothed themselves in fig leaves, and "hid themselves from the presence of the Lord" (Genesis 3:7-8). Just as seventeenth-century Puritan authors feared the tendency of language in art to become a Bablic monument of authorial self-idolatry, Bellamy treats language

Islands of Meaning 133

in his short story as a confusing babble signifying humanity's fall from some ideal; it is like clothing covering a nakedness of mind that humanity is ashamed to reveal. Everything in the story confirms this skeptical sense of language. At one point the narrator learns from the utopians that being able to speak is "an affliction," something so primitive that it is comparable to "the growling of animals" (pp. 393, 394). At another point the narrator notes that at best words communicate "imperfect descriptions of single thoughts" and, even worse, that words account for a profound "loneliness" because they cannot bridge the "gulf fixed between soul and soul" (pp. 401, 402).

"The impotence of words" (p. 404), the inability of language to communicate is one thing; its intrinsic predisposition to deceive is another. The narrator associates language with a "refuge of lies," a "foul cellar which taints the whole house above" (p. 404). Language is always, he says, an act of "concealment" (p. 404), an assertion echoing the various personae of seventeenth-century Puritan American writings. However, whereas most of these earlier narrators explore this concealment as potentially either a Satanic privation or a Christic plentitude of denotation, Bellamy's narrator stresses verbal obscurity as representative of the "veil of self" (p. 405), as an occlusion not only preventing one from sharing another's mind but also preventing one from penetrating one's own mind. "As a medium of self-revelation," the narrator explains, "speech is so inadequate and so misleading" (p. 406).

In this story words are equated to the fig-leaf clothing of Adam and Eve; words hide the shameful nakedness of a disgraceful egocentric mind, a situation that would be remedied in a renewed paradise where (to use the narrator's appropriated metaphor) the veil of self is rent. Words are also fittingly associated in the story with the human body. According to the Platonic and Christian traditions familiar to Bellamy, the body debasingly clothes and hides the naked soul. The human body, as the narrator pertinently observes, "is but the garment of a day" (p. 411). Words are like clothes and like the body: an external concealment (from others and from oneself) of an essential internal spiritual reality, or soul. In this story, then, words are a sign of humanity's fallen condition, a fall from some ideal state (like Eden); nevertheless, the narrator says, this human postlapsarian condition of obstructed communication can eventually become a paradise regained through a "universal human evolution which in time [is] destined to lead to the disuse of speech and the substitution of direct mental vision on the part of all races" (p. 394).

Such a view represents a major departure not only from the Puritan heritage of the dualistic potentiality of language but also from the later Emersonian and Transcendental heritage, which stressed the positive features of this heritage. As critics have noted,[30] Emersonian thought abides in Bellamy's writings. Transcendentalist ideas certainly seem present in "To Whom This May Come" when the narrator speaks of "the essential identity and being, the noumenal self, the core of the soul" that everyone mutually possesses (p. 411).[31] But in "To Whom This May Come" the view of language as a fallen medium is definitely not Emersonian and actually harkens back to a component of Puritan attitudes toward verbal expression. For Emerson, words are pictures, signs, or symbols of material facts; and in turn material facts are signs or symbols of spiritual facts.[32] Words might be a step removed from spiritual facts, but they embody them pictorially even as do features of nature. Although Emerson and the Transcendentalists understood that verbal expression was not one with the spirit informing it and although they sometimes worried about the possible rigidity of written discourse, they nonetheless invested an enormous amount of energy in using language as a tool of the self to link it (as Walt Whitman's "Noiseless Patient Spider" indicates) to other selves and things in the world.[33] Transcendental *logoi* were always *finally* potentially transformative in urging humanity to ascend collectively, as Emerson indicates in *The American Scholar* (1837), which argues that everything "aspire[s] to the highest" in accord with a natural (positive Babel-like) upward spiral ascent.[34]

In "To Whom This May Come" Bellamy couples this Romantic spiral of ascent with the social Darwinism of his day when his narrator speaks of "the higher, sun-bathed reaches of the upward path [humanity] plod[s]" (p. 415). And similarly in having the narrator refer to the utopians as "lords of themselves" who give true expression to "the noumenal self," Bellamy again yokes Transcendentalist thought and the social gospel of his day, especially the notions popularized by Englishman Herbert Spenser and American John Fiske, who argued that human consciousness and ethics would evolve ever higher until human civilization achieved a utopian order and stability. But on the specific issue of language in "To Whom This May Come," Bellamy departs distinctly from his Emersonian and social Darwinian predecessors, and apparently echoes the darker side of the Puritan tradition in which he was raised.

Bellamy's attack on language could have been influenced by several other sources. Wilhelm Friedrich Nietzsche is an unlikely choice, as is Arthur Schopenhauer, whose attack on ideation and language as perpetuators of human misery had a profound effect on several of the writers of Bellamy's time.[35] More likely the influence of Hawthorne and (possibly) of Melville—both also wrestling with features of their Puritan heritage—figured in Bellamy's formulation about words in "To Whom They May Come." These two authors frequently attacked the Transcendental idea of language as a sacred conductor of higher meaning. Moreover, in the nineteenth century such other American writers as Byron Johnson and Horace Bushnell emphasized the indeterminateness of language, both its tendency toward ambiguity and its inability to penetrate beyond the restrictions of the senses.[36] In *Mardi* (1849) Melville provides the startling proposition that "words are but algebraic signs, conveying no meaning except what you please," that words are "mere substitutions of sounds for inexplicable meanings."[37] In *The Scarlet Letter* (1850) Hawthorne creates an ambiguity about the letter A, which comes to represent several possible meanings (angel, able, adulterer, among others), and about Hester, the wearer of that A, who might be seen as reprehensible or praiseworthy depending on the reader's perspective. By problematizing the first letter of the alphabet in

The Scarlet Letter, Hawthorne slyly raises questions about the nature and significance (sign value) of language, including that of his romance, as a conductor of certifiable meaning. Language, at once seeming to reveal even while it conceals meaning—in part because humanity is trapped in a relentless interpretative subjectivity—is a common concern in Hawthorne's stories,[38] as it is in the Puritan heritage that fascinated Hawthorne. In his fiction, as in the writings of his Puritan predecessors, the connotative ambiguities of the logogic crux vex any attempt to derive certain allegorical readings of Hawthorne's *ostensibly* allegorical short stories.

Wherever Bellamy might have found authority to condemn language so rigorously, the attack on words in "To Whom This May Come" repudiates the Emersonian and Transcendentalist authority they seem to have in most of *Looking Backward,* which is virtually a dialogue. In this novel there is an abundance of "social intercourse," and there are plenty of books, writers, and a library.[39]

Nevertheless, the novel specifically deplores "shameless self-assertion and mutual depreciation,"[40] a mere hint perhaps at the discontent with the essential capabilities of language Bellamy would express in "To Whom This May Come," published a year after the novel's appearance. There are other traces as well of this discontent in *Looking Backward.* In his dream return to Boston near the end of the romance, Julian's words fail to persuade his hearers of the benefits of utopianism. Similarly, at the fringe of the reader's consciousness, a question is raised about whether Julian himself would have been converted to utopianism had not his experiences, particularly his enjoyment of Edith's love, reinforced Dr. Leete's words. Problematic too is a remark made by Julian (speaking here for Bellamy) concerning the limitations of the nineteenth-century romance tradition compared to the "different . . . course" taken in Berians's utopian work.[41]

These moments comprise small, if noteworthy, countercurrents in a work that implies at heart a positive view of language. After the publication of *Looking Backward,* however, Bellamy seems to hesitate more deliberately over the essentially Transcendentalist notion of the transformative power of language that informs the very matrix of his novel.

One reason why Bellamy's hesitation over language increased in 1888 was probably inaccessible to him. Fearful of labor unrest and of social violence, he must have felt ambivalent over the socialism at the heart of his novel. At some level of his mind this ambivalence might have augmented his sense of the duplicity of language, specifically his own language, as something that simultaneously reveals and conceals.

A second reason for Bellamy's uneasiness in 1888 about language might be found in the fact that *Looking Backward* is a romance, the original design of which Bellamy clearly remembered as "a mere literary fantasy, a fairy tale" with "no idea of . . . a serious contribution to the movement of social reform." Bellamy admits this origin in an article published in May 1889, seventeen months after the publication of the novel; but by this time he has begun to reconstruct those origins, and he readily cloaks both his initial admission about origination and the remarks that he "stumbled over the destined corner-stone of the new social order" with the assurance that finally he had converted this "fairy tale of social perfection" into "the vehicle of a definite scheme of industrial reorganization."[42] Later, in April 1894, he would publish another article on the same subject that further reconstructs the origins of his novel and that completely evades any confession of the questionable positioning of that work within the genre of romance.[43] As the years passed, Bellamy continued to reconceive the original design behind *Looking Backward*, but during the year after its publication, before sales boomed and the first Nationalist Club was organized, he apparently was less comfortable over a too literal reading of his romance. The fantasy or fairy tale genre of romance, Bellamy knew, employs language expansively, even allegorically, to convey intimated, not literal meanings.

A third likely reason why Bellamy hesitated in 1888 over the nature of language might have been at the forefront of his mind when he wrote "To Whom This May Come": the reviews *Looking Backward* received. That novel was eventually a sensation, selling over 160,000 copies in two years and exerting a great influence.⁴⁴ But such success was not the case during the first year after the publication of the novel, which sold a mere 10,000 copies during 1888.⁴⁵ Nevertheless, there were reviews and discussions of the book, some favorable, some picking away at this or that point, some negative. Whereas, for example, the review in the *New York Tribune* (5 February 1888) praised the book as a brilliant artistic success, the review in the London *Saturday Review* (24 March 1888) dismissed it as dull and stupid.⁴⁶ Reviews like the one in the *New York Tribune* notwithstanding, Bellamy pondered the reception of his romance and apparently confronted two facts: that intrinsically language is limited in its capacity to communicate any vision and that extrinsically people, both those for and against his book, tend to focus narrowly on the literal words on the page rather than tend to perceive, at a higher level of insight, the spirit behind those words. In spite of some exceptions, too many readers of his romance, so sluggish in sales while he was writing "To Whom This May Come," might have seemed to him to have attended more to the linguistic clothes or body of his text rather than to the mind or soul within it.

Interestingly, this metaphor informing "To Whom This May Come" occurs as well in the favorable review in the *New York Tribune*. This review describes Bellamy as a "prose writer" who shows "a power beyond that of poetry, for he has so clothed his conceptions with the garment of realism that they appear to us no longer distant and unattainable shadows."⁴⁷ In "To Whom This May Come" Bellamy seizes this metaphor to make precisely the opposite point: that the lingual garment of representation can indeed overshadow conceptions. Bellamy might have felt that such an overshadowing had indeed occurred in the instance of those reviewers who focused on one or another specific idea or detail rather than reacted to his book as a whole.

In this context it is probable that "To Whom This May Come" represents a reply to the nit-picking reviewers of *Looking Backward* and an admonition to its admirers as well. This short story is apparently an allegory about the need to read Bellamy's romance, as it were, telepathically for the spirit of

Islands of Meaning 139

its meaning rather than literally for the clothes or the body comprised of the specific language of its recommendations. Indeed, such a view of a Bellamian text is encouraged by a metaphor seized upon by the narrator of the short story when he says that among the utopians his "mind was an open book" to "be judged with . . . fairness and . . . sympathy" (p. 403). The trouble with *Looking Backward*, viewed in retrospect by Bellamy, might have been that it made him feel uncomfortable at some unconscious level of his mind because of its "stumbling" romance origins as well as its ambivalence-producing socialistic vision; at a more conscious level of his mind, he sensed perhaps that too many of his critics had opened his book and found the letter of his words (specific connotations) without finding the spirit of his mind (visionary denotation). Somehow, he apparently felt, the language of that work failed to disclose the spirit of his mind as if it were an open book.

The overarching allegorical intention behind the plot, the religious allusions, and (as we shall see) the narrational manner of "To Whom This May Come" is, then, possibly aimed at the instruction of Bellamy's audience about a higher mode of reading his logogic sites, a way of reading *through* the clothing-like embodiment of language—rending the veil of the egocentric author and reader alike—to discover its soul-like meaning. And the key to this allegorical intention, one that neatly combines the plot about telepathy and the religious allusions, can be found in 2 Corinthians 3:6: "Who also hath made us able ministers of the new testament; not of the letter, but of the spirit: for the letter killeth, but the spirit giveth life." In this passage Paul emphasizes Jesus' reformation of the Jewish adherence to the letter of Mosaic law. Jesus replaced the decalogue with merely two commandments: love of God and love of one's neighbor; and Bellamy's entire career was devoted to arguing that altruism towards one's neighbor expresses one's love of God, who (in Bellamy's "Religion of Solidarity") is a Transcendentalistic "All-soul" and who resides within all humanity, making everyone theosophical brothers and sisters.[48] Moreover, Jesus spoke in allegories presumably because he wanted to frustrate a slavishly literal reading of his own pronouncements and to encourage a continual search for the spirit of the meaning they allegorically embody. In this passage in 2 Corinthians Paul summarizes the essential message of Jesus' teaching, a message concerning the need to abandon a legalistic, *literal* approach to religious belief (which in Pauline and Calvinistic Christianity will save no one) for an experience of the *spirit* of that belief.

Bellamy, who read the Bible even through his last years, certainly knew this Pauline message well, especially since his youth was saturated by Christianity in the Calvinist tradition. Puritan tradition was profoundly informed by this Pauline message in its emphasis on the spirit of hope over reasoned security, a central feature of the Puritan author's management of logogic sites as a potential intersection of the eternal and the temporal.

This essential Pauline component of Bellamy's Puritan heritage aptly applies to his sense of his own latter-day new testament concerning the evolution of humanity toward a millennial utopian realization of a paradise regained on earth.[49] Like Jesus' reliance on allegory, Bellamy used this mode of discourse to convey a visionary message about the possibility of a new spirit; and like Jesus (whom Bellamy saw as an exemplary humanistic social reformer), Bellamy initially resisted what he apparently perceived to be the tendency of his audience to take too literal an approach to his work, as so many who had argued over specific details in *Looking Backward* seemed to have done.

When Cyrus Field Willard wrote to him, shortly after the appearance of *Looking Backward*, about promoting the ideas expressed in this book, Bellamy was surprised and pleased; but in a letter of 4 July 1888, in response to Willard's desire to form the Nationalist Club, Bellamy was oddly cool: "Go ahead by all means and do it if you can find anybody to associate with."[50] Bellamy's enthusiasm for the Nationalist movement grew a year *after* the publication of *Looking Backward*, when sales of the book finally began to increase and when the club actually became organized. During the year 1888, however, Bellamy seems to have hesitated over a too literal approach to

Islands of Meaning 141

his romance by his detractors and his supporters, the latter possibly threatening to institutionalize the novel as if it were a new scripture. Just as Paul indicated that a strict adherence to the letter of the law leads to failure (spiritual death), Bellamy apparently fretted over how too restrictive an adherence to the literal specifics, the Bablic connotative dimension, of the words of his novel might lead to the failure of its message about the need for a denotative new spirit.

Bellamy had aimed for an inspirational, even religious, encouragement of the mind of his readers, who would, he hoped, be moved to respond to his millennial utopian prophecy not principally in terms of a rational analysis of its literal details (which were certainly open to argument) but in terms of conversionlike emotion, sympathetic feeling, metamorphic spirit. The spirit has priority over the literal or pragmatic because, Bellamy believed in accord with the Puritan notion of conversion, human mental attitudes must change before material reality can be modified. People must first have faith and hope, as in the conservative Puritan stress on justification before sanctification, before salvation is possible; then a mutation in empirical reality will follow. As the narrator of Bellamy's story says, alterations in the mind produce alterations in the material world: "reaction[s occur] upon the body [from an] ideal mental and moral health and placidity" (p. 409).

That the actual literal words (*embodying* spirit or mind) are no more important than is someone's physical appearance to the utopian islanders (who perceive only the minds of their neighbors [pp. 408-409]) is reinforced by the narrative manner of Bellamy's short story. At the beginning of the account the narrator tells of his near death in a storm at sea that is almost biblically apocalyptic: "I gave myself up for lost, and was indeed already past the worst of drowning" (p. 389). This passage applies the Christian notion that one must lie down (die) before he or she can rise up (eternal life), and it intimates that the old self of nineteenth-century literal reality must die for the new self of utopian possibility to emerge. At the end of the story the narrator is once again threatened by death at sea, and this time he does indeed die, willingly because he cannot endure the reality of the world of egocentric babble to which he has returned. Like the utopians, he looks to the world after death as merely a fuller realization of the human capacity to live in the spirit rather than to live only literally: "The life of the mind-readers while yet they are in the body is so largely spiritual that the idea of an existence wholly so, which seems vague and chill to us, suggests to them a state only slightly more refined than they already know on earth" (p. 414).

The narrator's demise is appropriate not only because it suggests allegorically that the old self must expire to make way for the birth of a new self, but also because he has *written* his account, a metaphoric feature of which indicates, first, that words (a fallen babble) are utterly inadequate to communicate visionary spirit and, second, that the very literalness of these words can *kill* the meaning or significance of their message. The narrator's death is a final allegorical sign in the story to make the point that "the letter killeth," that just as (in Calvinist dogma) the postlapsarian body can condemn its soul to eternal death, so too a literal, Bablic reading of a prophetic visionary work like Bellamy's can result in the demise of the "new-testament" spirit of its allegorical message.[51]

The terminal note appended by E.B. only reinforces this sense. E.B. says simply: "The extent of my own connection with the foregoing document is sufficiently indicated by the author himself in the final paragraph" (p. 415). There are two important features to remark in this passage. First, unlike most nineteenth-century stories with a frame narrator, E.B. has not introduced himself at the beginning or at the end of the narrative proper, but confines himself to an utterly marginal voice in a single-sentence footnote to the narrative. This self-effacing manner draws no egocentric attention to E .B. (which fact keeps the note in harmony with the humanistic message of the story) and becomes a virtual silence forcing the reader mentally to drift back to the narrative for bearings. Second, E.B.'s note instructs the reader to return to the final paragraph of the account, the paragraph with the passage about the narrator's desire "for hope's sake" that readers will see in the story a "glimpse of the higher sunbathed reaches of the upward path

Islands of Meaning 143

they trod" (p. 415). In this final paragraph the story (plot) dies, the voice (allusion, language) dies, the narrator (narrative manner) dies—each signifying that "the letter killeth." This dying away of everything in the story suggests that its meaning, its denotative significance, cannot finally be found in the mutable, unstable mortal corporeality of the text. The meaning of the story resides in the noumenal silence bounding the text of the narrative and the text of any "apparent self." In this noumenal silence ideally "the core of the soul" of the narrator, of E.B., and of the reader can sympathetically or telepathically communicate denotatively with each other as if each were "an open book:" The dying into silence of plot, allusion, and narrative manner in the last paragraph of the story suits Bellamy's allegorical purpose. This pattern expresses Bellamy's wish that in the contemplative silence of the reader's mind, plunged into the silence into which the story itself falls, the reader will sympathetically sense (as in a religious conversion experience) an understanding (denotation) transcending the linguistic literalness (connotation) so inadequate to the communication of visionary ideational meaning. This technique is very similar, as we noted in chapter 4, to Edwards's assault on language in order to intimate the difference between *sciential* knowledge and saving *sapiential* apprehension of reality. Bellamy also smashes words in repudiation of their tendency to form iconic monuments luring humanity into an idolatrous worship of the temporal limitations of human reason. Bellamy envisions an ideal union of his and his readers' minds in a noumenal silence beyond the material world and its verbal graven images, a union corresponding to the spiritual life after physical death posited by the utopians in the short story. Then the significance of the author's prophetic message about the human capacity for a potential spiritual transformation of material reality into a millennial utopia might live in spirit rather than be killed by the obscuring literalness of words.

In paradoxically using words to attack the efficacy of language, a darker feature of Bellamy's Puritan and Hawthornian heritage, "To Whom This May Come" seems to be a self-reflexive allegory about the Bellamian use of allegory, at least as he assessed it in 1888. Possibly responding to the critics of *Looking Backward*, Bellamy's short story, amplifying 2 Corinthians 3:6, combines a plot about telepathy, religious and scriptural allusions, and narrative technique to instruct his readers on how to read his "new-testament" allegories of millennial utopianism. He instructs his audience to avoid a slavish rational adherence to the literal words of his texts, which (if we apply Morton's metaphor) are like a Trojan horse. This surface verbiage of plot and detail is, in Bellamy's terms, only like clothing concealing the body or like the body hiding the soul. Similar to the body in relation to the soul in Calvinist theology and to the Puritan author who worried that words might indict rather than exonerate the writer, verbal exteriors, in Bellamy's opinion, can lead to the death of the very ideas about human possibilities they try to express. He urges his audience to read with feeling, with (as if ready for a conversion experience) a heart open to the influx of the spirit of the denotative visionary ideational message embodied or *enclothed* or concealed in his allegorical logogic sites. For the transcendent, transformative spirit that (in Paul's words) "giveth life" is, for Bellamy, ideally to be received and appreciated (like the grace of the Holy Spirit), not rationally (in accord with the literalness or letter of dogma) but sympathetically, in faith and hope, as if through a utopian telepathic bond between author and reader.

Like Fiske's allegory, Bellamy's story intertwines the historical and the allegorical into a Gordian knot. When Fiske's essay entangles the reader in twisted double-talk and when Bellamy's tale uses allegory reflexively to demystify the language of allegory, they both conceal their respective author's temporal artistry within an *intimated* higher aesthetic vision, one that teasingly remains inaccessible to the reader. Both works ultimately indicate the circumstantial nature of Bablic verbal autonomy, replete with obscure connotative corruptions of any humanly envisioned denotative meaning. But whereas Fiske's potentially satiric essay reveals the human difficulty of finding any definitive meaning at the logogic site itself, Bellamy's angry narrative expresses the sentiment of the iconoclast who deplores the displacement of denotative referentiality in human language. Finally, unlike the example of seventeenth-century Puritan literature, Fiske's and Bellamy's logogic cruxes do not suggest that some divine revelation paradoxically and obscurely intermingles with the ephemeral signs of the temporal world. Rather, both of their works leave the reader stymied before the puzzling nature of language itself.

In contrast to early American Puritan practice, then, Fiske and Bellamy cannot exploit the dynamic tension of the doubletalk of human discourse in a way that ultimately implies a divine authority behind language. In emphasizing the logogic crux, Fiske's essay and Bellamy's story both suggest that language is apparently disempowered in the matter of conveying definitive meaning, that what it principally conceals allegorically is not something eternal but rather only its capacity for conveying an illusion of closure with some ultimate referentiality. Unlike their seventeenth-century Puritan predecessors, neither author enjoys the *full* invigorating dualistic heritage of Renaissance and Reformed concepts pertaining to the nature of words. On the contrary, their logogic sites are like the islands in their allegories: places once historically connected to a heritage of allegorical temporal existence. Inadvertently, Fiske plays, albeit very obscurely, at the logogic site, in contrast to the example of a Puritan humorist like Nathaniel Ward; Bellamy, on the other hand, cannot play at the verbal site any more than could Edwards. Bellamy lacks the empowering authority of a nervous appreciation, like that of the early colonial Puritans, of how eternal truth may be concealed within the Bablic dispersion of this truth in the riot of a human language that has fallen into temporal connotations; and, consequently, in "To Whom This May Come" Bellamy prefers silence, a muteness not to be redeemed into voice in any way similar to that found by Anne Bradstreet and Edward Taylor. For Bellamy, at least in 1888, the word had become *entzaubert* (to apply Max Weber's famous neologism): the wonder had departed from it. For Bellamy, the thrill of the fear and hope that his Puritan predecessors had felt at the logogic site was gone.

Notes

Introduction

1. J. Hillis Miller, "The Function of Literary Theory at the Present Time," *The Future of Literary Theory*, ed. Ralph Cohen (New York: Routledge, 1989), pp. 102-11.
2. Dominick LaCapra, *Rethinking Intellectual History: Texts, Contexts, Language* (Ithaca: Cornell Univ. Press, 1983), pp. 36-56.
3. For the theoretical rationale for the multivolume *Le Lieux de mémoire*, published in France at different times during the 1980s and 1990s, see Pierre Nora, "Between Memory and History: *Les Lieux de Mémoire*," *Representations* 26 (1989): 7-25.
4. Samuel Mather, *The Figures or Types of the Old Testament* (London, 1673), pp. 58-59.
5. This issue is, for example, raised by William C. Spengemann, *A Mirror for Americanists: Reflections on the Idea of American Literature* (Hanover: Univ. Press of New England, 1989) and implied by David Hackett Fischer, *Albion's Seed: Four British Folkways in America* (New York: Oxford Univ. Press, 1989).

1. The Necessity of Language

1. "Governour Bradford's Letter Book," *Collections of the Massachusetts Historical Society* 3 (1794): 37-38. An earlier version of several of my observations here appeared as "The Theme of Necessity in Bradford's *Of Plymouth Plantation*," *Seventeenth-Century News* 32 (1974): 88-90.
2. *Of Plymouth Plantation*, ed. Samuel Eliot Morison (New York: Knopf, 1952), pp. 118-19.
3. Peter Gay, *A Loss of Mastery: Puritan Historians in Colonial America* (New York: Vintage, 1968), pp. 46-47.
4. Alan B. Howard, "Art and History in Bradford's *Of Plymouth Plantation*," *William and Mary Quarterly*, 28 (1971), 245-46. In "'With

My Owne Eyes'": William Bradford's *Of Plymouth Plantation"* (*Typology and Early American Literature*, ed. Sacvan Bercovitch [Amherst: Univ. of Massachusetts Press, 1972], pp. 95-98) Jasper Rosenmeier interprets this providential pattern in the first book of the history as a typological reenactment of Christ's death and resurrection.

5. "A Descriptive and Historical Account of New England in Verse," *Publications of the Massachusetts Historical Society* 11 (1870): 468.

6. "[Epitaphium Meum"], *American Poetry of the Seventeenth Century*, ed. Harrison T. Meserole (University Park: Pennsylvania State Univ. Press, 1985), p. 390.

7. This image of Plymouth appears as well in "A Descriptive and Historical Account," pp. 473, 474, 477. A revisionist reading of this correspondence between New England and Israel is provided by Theodore Dwight Bozeman, *To Live Ancient Lives: The Primitivist Dimension in Puritanism* (Chapel Hill: North Carolina Univ. Press, 1988).

8. See Bradford Smith, *Bradford of Plymouth* (Philadelphia: Lippincott, 1951), pp. 187-88.

9. In "A Dialogue or Third Conference" Bradford particularly emphasizes the love and loyalty cementing the community of the Independents (*Publications of the Massachusetts Historical Society* 11 (1870): 462-63.

10. "So vain is man! if riches do abide / A little, he's soon lift up with pride" ("A Descriptive and Historical Account," p. 470). The role of pride is also treated in Bradford's "A Word to New England" and "Of Boston in New England" (*American Poetry of the Seventeenth Century*, pp. 387-89).

11. See, for example, Norman S. Grabo, "William Bradford: *Of Plymouth Plantation*" in *Landmarks of American Writing*, ed. Hennig Cohen (New York: Basic Books, 1969), p. 16; and John Griffith, "*Of Plymouth Plantation* as a Mercantile Epic," *Arizona Quarterly* 28 (1972): 237.

12. See, for instance, Robert Daly, "William Bradford's Vision of History," *American Literature* 44 (1973): 566. William Haller merely notes a shift in Bradford's interest, from the war against Satan to the practical problems of the colony: *The Rise of Puritanism* (New York: Harper and Row, 1957), p. 191; and E.F. Bradford emphasizes a cause-and-effect structural principle in the work: "Conscious Art in Bradford's *History of Plymouth Plantation*," *New England Quarterly* 1 (1928): 133-57.

13. Daly also considers the entry for 1632 as the decisive locus of Bradford's shift in vision (p. 564).

14. Compare "A Word to New Plymouth," *Publications of the Massachusetts Historical Society* 11 (1870): 428.

15. Daly, p. 568; David Levin, [review of *The Loss of Mastery*],

History and Theory 7 (1968): 393; Howard, p. 249; A. Carl Bredahl, Jr., *New Ground: Western American Narrative and the Literary Canon* (Chapel Hill: Univ. of North Carolina Press, 1989), pp. 8-28.

16. Donald F. Connors, "Thomas Morton of Merry Mount: His First Arrival in New England," *American Literature* 11 (1939): 160-66.

17. On this contrast, see Donald F. Connors, *Thomas Morton* (New York: Twayne, 1969), p. 132.

18. Thomas Morton, *New English Canaan* (Amsterdam: J.F. Stam, 1637), p. 57. My comments on Morton are based on my "Morton's *New English Canaan*," *Explicator* 31, vi (1973): 47, as permitted by the Helen Dwight Reed Educational Foundation.

19. Daniel B. Shea, "'Our Professed Old Adversary': Thomas Morton and the Naming of New England," *Early American Literature* 23 (1988): 52-69.

20. See Robert D. Arner, "Mythology and the Maypole of Merrymount: Some Notes on Thomas Morton's 'Rise Oedipus,'" *Early American Literature* 6 (1971): 156-64.

21. For a cogent defense of Miller against the charge of an overemphasis on intellectual matters and of a distorted and monolithic reading of Puritan culture, see Francis T. Butts, "Norman Fiering and the Revision of Perry Miller," *Canadian Review of American Studies* 17 (1986): 1-26.

22. Perry Miller, *The New England Mind: The Seventeenth Century* (Boston: Beacon Press, 1961), p. 307.

23. On the Puritan sense of the limits and proper uses of reason, see John Morgan, *Godly Learning: Puritan Attitudes towards Reason, Learning, and Education, 1560-1640* (Cambridge: Cambridge Univ. Press, 1986), pp. 41-61. On the Scholastic logicians' perception of a gap between speech and thought—a perception that did not eliminate their ideal of linguistic transparency—and on the Renaissance thinkers' attempt to close this gap, see Martin Elsky, *Authorizing Words: Speech, Writing, and Print in the English Renaissance* (Ithaca: Cornell Univ. Press, 1990).

24. David Quint, *Origin and Originality in Renaissance Literature: Versions of the Source* (New Haven: Yale Univ. Press, 1983).

25. Miller, pp. 305-6.

26. In *The Estrangement of the Past: A Study in the Origins of Modern Historical Consciousness* (New York: Oxford Univ. Press, 1990) Anthony M. Kemp attributes the historical consciousness of dynamic temporality to the Reformation experience of revolution and supercession, which created a great schism in the fabric of the static Renaissance world view. Although this conclusion is not compatible to my understanding of the Renaissance, Kemp's sense of the dualism of subsequent Reformed histories is pertinent to my discussion. Kemp's appreciation of the paradoxical struggle of these writers to at once celebrate the changes of time and reestablish the stasis of essential truth supports my point about the logogic site as a nexus of the temporal and the eternal.

27. See William J. Scheick, *The Will and the Word: The Poetry of Edward Taylor* (Athens: Univ. of Georgia Press, 1974), pp. 5-8.

28. The Puritan trouble with the referential function of words is remarked by Michael Clark, "The Honeyed Knot of Puritan Aesthetics," *Puritan Poets and Poetics: Seventeenth-Century American Poetry in Theory and Practice*, ed. Peter White (University Park: Pennsylvania State Univ. Press, 1985), pp. 67-83.

29. *American Poetry of the Seventeenth Century*, p. 486.

30. Saint Augustine, *On Free Choice of the Will*, trans. Anna S. Benjamin and L.H. Hackstaff (Indianapolis: Bobbs-Merrrrill, 1964), p. 74.

31. Marcia L. Colish, *The Mirror of Language: A Study in the Medieval Theory of Knowledge* (Lincoln: Univ. of Nebraska Press, 1983), pp. 7-54.

32. On the nature of the sacramentality of the sermonic word as a facilitator of grace and a ritualistic transformer of everyday experience into divine meaning, see Harry S. Stout, *The New England Soul: Preaching and Religious Culture in Colonial New England* (New York: Oxford Univ. Press, 1986).

33. *The Poems of Edward Taylor*, ed. Donald E. Stanford (New Haven: Yale Univ. Press, 1960), pp. 17, 239.

34. Components of Puritan beliefs that enabled the authorization of art are noted by Robert Daly, *God's Altar: The World and the Flesh in Puritan Poetry* (Berkeley: Univ. of California Press, 1978), pp. 40-81; on Taylor's extensive Augustinian heritage, see Scheick, *The Will and the Word*.

35. *Two Mather Biographies: "Life and Death" and "Parentator,"* ed. William J. Scheick (Bethlehem: Lehigh Univ. Press, 1989), pp. 60-61.

36. See "Anonymity and Signature," *Two Mather Biographies*, pp. 11-21.

37. See, for example, Wayne Rebhorn, *Courtly Performances: Masking and Festivity in Castiglione's "Book of the Courtier"* (Detroit: Wayne State Univ. Press, 1978), pp. 31-33; Miller, p. 324.

38. *The Puritans: A Sourcebook of Their Writings*, ed. Perry Miller and Thomas H. Johnson (New York: Harper, 1963), 2:672.

39. On the probable nature of this audience, see Michael Colacurcio, "*Gods Determinations Touching Half-Way Membership:* Occasion and Audience in Edward Taylor," *American Literature* 39 (1967): 298-314; and J. Daniel Patterson, "*Gods Determinations:* The Occasion and the Audience, and Taylor's Hope for New England," *Early American Literature* 22 (1987): 63-81. On the specifically instructional nature of Ramist rhetoric, see Walter J. Ong, *Ramus: Method, and the Decay of Dialogue* (Cambridge: Harvard Univ. Press, 1958), pp. 273-75. On the pattern of oppositions in Taylor's poem, see William J. Scheick, "The Jawbones Scheme of Edward Taylor's *God's Determinations*," *Puritan Influences in American Literature*, ed. Emory Elliott (Urbana: Univ. of Illinois Press, 1979), pp. 38-54, from which I have drawn for some of my commentary at this point in my discussion. On the tension

between artistic impulse and scriptural authority in Taylor's poem, see Lynn M. Haims, "Puritan Iconography: The Art of Edward Taylor's *Gods Determinations*," *Puritan Poets and Poetics*, pp. 84-98.
   40. *The Poems of Edward Taylor*, p. 399.
   41. *Edward Taylor's Christographia*, ed. Norman S. Grabo (New Haven: Yale Univ. Press, 1962), pp. 117, 24-25, 96.
   42. *The Works of Anne Bradstreet*, ed. Jeannine Hensley (Cambridge: Harvard Univ. Press, 1967), pp. 206-7; *The Poems of Edward Taylor*, p. 35.

2. The Winding Sheet of Meditative Verse

   1. Thomas H. Johnson, "Edward Taylor: A Puritan 'Sacred Poet,'" *New England Quarterly* 10 (1937): 290-322.
   2. The course of studies on Bradstreet's verse is detailed in Raymond F. Dolle, *Anne Bradstreet: A Reference Guide* (Boston: G.K. Hall, 1990); and on Taylor's verse is detailed in William J. Scheick and JoElla Doggett, *Seventeenth-Century American Poetry: A Reference Guide* (Boston: G.K. Hall, 1977); in Catherine Rainwater and William J. Scheick, "Seventeenth-Century American Poetry: A Reference Guide Updated," *Resources for American Literary Study* 10 (1980): 121-45; and (for supplemental entries) Scheick, "Literature to 1800," in the volumes of *American Literary Scholarship* (Durham: Duke Univ. Press) for the years 1978 to 1988.
   3. See Michael McGiffert, "American Puritan Studies in the 1960's," *William and Mary Quarterly* 27 (1970): 36-67; and E. Brooks Holifield, *The Covenant Sealed: The Development of Puritan Sacramental Theology in Old and New England, 1570-1720* (New Haven: Yale Univ. Press, 1974).
   4. Barbara Kiefer Lewalski, "Edward Taylor: Lisp of Praise and Strategies for Self-Dispraise," *Protestant Poetics and the Seventeenth-Century Religious Lyric* (Princeton: Princeton Univ. Press, 1979), pp. 388-426.
   5. Alan Howard, "The World as Emblem: Language and Vision in the Poetry of Edward Taylor," *American Literature* 44 (1972): 359-84.
   6. Karen Rowe, *Saint and Singer: Edward Taylor's Typology and the Poetics of Meditation* (Cambridge: Cambridge Univ. Press, 1986), pp. 125, 47, 270.
   7. John Gatta, *Gracious Laughter: The Meditative Wit of Edward Taylor* (Columbia: Univ. of Missouri Press, 1989), pp. 8, 11, 207.
   8. See, representatively, Karl Keller, *The Example of Edward Taylor* (Amherst: Univ. of Massachusetts Press, 1975), pp. 161-88.
   9. John McWilliams, "Writing Literary History: The Limits of Nationalism," *Resources for American Literary Study* 13 (1983): 127-33.
   10. Alan Leander MacGregor, "Edward Taylor and the Impertinent Metaphor," *American Literature* 60 (1988): 337-58. For a de-

constructive reading of Taylor, see Michael Clark's "The Honeyed Knot of Puritan Aesthetics," *Puritan Poets and Poetics: Seventeenth-Century American Poetry in Theory and Practice,* ed. Peter White (University Park: Pennsylvania State Univ. Press, 1985), pp. 67-83. Clark argues that Taylor cancels the sensible bases of language by disrupting the integrity of language as a sign, which disruption allows for the revelation of a more ultimate sign.

11. See, for example, Josephine K. Piercy, *Anne Bradstreet* (New York: Twayne, 1965).

12. See, for example, Robert D. Richardson, "The Puritan Poetry of Anne Bradstreet," *Texas Studies in Literature and Language* 9 (1967): 317-31; and Anne Hildebrand, "Anne Bradstreet's Quaternions and 'Contemplations,'" *Early American Literature* 8 (1973): 117-25.

13. Statements about the artistry of this poem tend to be general or, as in the instance of Alvin H. Rosenfeld's "Anne Bradstreet's 'Contemplations': Patterns of Form and Meaning" (*New England Quarterly* 43 [1970]: 79-96), have emphasized such obvious matters as unifying imagery based on the seasonal and diurnal cycles, as good use of classical and biblical allusions, and as a harmonious integration of mood, tone, and setting.

14. In *Anne Bradstreet: The Wordly Puritan* (New York: Burt Franklin, 1974 [pp. 93-106]), Ann Stanford notes the pertinence of emblematic tradition in "Contemplations," but sidesteps the issue to discuss meditative tradition in the poem.

15. Anthony Burgess, "Native Ground," *The Atlantic* 261 (Jan. 1988): 89.

16. William J. Scheick, "'The Inward Tacles and the Outward Traces': Edward Taylor's Elusive Transitions," *Early American Literature* 12 (1977): 163-76.

17. Recent feminist reassessments of Bradstreet's verse sometimes remark that certain distortions in her poetry represent her conscious revision of male poetic conventions; see, for example, Ivy Schweitzer, "Anne Bradstreet Wrestles with the Renaissance," *Early American Literature* 23 (1989): 291-312.

18. All quotations from Bradstreet's verse derive from *The Works of Anne Bradstreet,* ed. Jeannine Hensley (Cambridge: Harvard Univ. Press, 1967). An earlier version of my comments here appeared as "The Theme, Structure, and Symbolism of Anne Bradstreet's 'Contemplations,'" *Américana* 4 (1989): 147-56.

19. The dialectical conflict in the poem between an attraction to the world (lyricism) and a theologically dictated renunciation of the world (meditation) is best documented by Richardson and Rosenfeld.

20. Attempts, modest at best, to define the structure of this poem include: a thematic integration of the whole work (Piercy, Richardson, and Rosenfeld); a scheme based on fire, earth, water and air (Eberwein); and a progression from statement of subject and description of scene, through analysis, to moral truth—a progression characteristic of the meditative tradition (Stanford).

21. Critics, on the whole, have been too ready to read a proto-Romanticism into "Contemplations." Elizabeth Wade White implies this reading when she says that in this poem "the effect of the whole is that of a symphonic meditation attuned to nature's music" (*Anne Bradstreet: "The Tenth Muse"* [New York: Oxford Univ. Press, 1971], p. 336), when in fact the poet specifically says that she cannot tune her art to even approach the successful music of abject insects. More overt are Piercy's claims as developed by Rosenfeld, who acknowledges certain Christian limitations observed by the poet but who indicates that her poem shares with Romantic verse a consolation for humans derived from the seasonal cycles; in fact the poet says clearly that the trees are "insensible of time," while mankind "grows old, lies down, remains where once he's laid" because for mankind nothing will (the poet puns) "spring again" (lines, 122, 126, 131). In "Anne Bradstreet's Use of DuBartas in 'Contemplations,'" *Essex Institute Historical Collections* 110 (1974): 64-69, Kenneth A. Requa indicates that the application of Romantic concepts to this poem needs qualification; in "Religious Tension in the Poetry of Anne Bradstreet," *Christianity and Literature* 25, ii (1976): 30-36, Robert C. Wess suggests that the poet anticipates the Romantic delight in nature itself.

22. In "The Wounds Upon Bathsheba: Anne Bradstreet's Prophetic Art," in *Puritan Poets and Poetics*, pp. 136, Rosamond R. Rosenmeier observes, interestingly, that the poet's retreat from silence into the past follows the pattern of the poet in Psalm 44.

23. In "Allegory and Typology 'Imbrace and Greet': Anne Bradstreet's 'Contemplations,'" *Early American Literature* 10 (1975): 30-46, William J. Irvin suggests that in the poem the river symbolizes the earthly pilgrimage of the soul as it seeks heaven.

24. The importance of humility as a recurrent theme in Bradstreet's verse is remarked by Kenneth R. Ball, "Puritan Humility in Anne Bradstreet's Poetry," *Cithara* 13, i (1973): 29-41. The poet's conscious manipulation of conventional poetic formulae concerning humility is the subject of Eileen Margerum's "Anne Bradstreet's Public Poetry and the Tradition of Humility," *Early American Literature* 17 (1982): 152-60.

25. On the Augustinian heritage behind the inclusion of the temporal order within the divine, see Scheick, *The Will and the Word*, pp. 8-17. An earlier version of my comments here appeared as "Unfolding the Serpent in Taylor's 'Meditation 1.19,'" *Studies in Puritan American Spirituality* 1 (1990): 34-64.

26. Quotations from "Meditation 1.19" are cited from Stanford, *The Poems of Edward Taylor*, pp 32-33. My only change is the preservation of the manuscript word "mikewhite," which in this edition has been emended to read "milkwhite" (line 9). While this alteration is reasonable, it obscures Taylor's possible intention to suggest that the Lamb of God is not only milkwhite but also *makes* white the redeemed saints—that is, transforms their sickly pallor into a restored innocent whiteness. In this way, the Lamb is a *mike*, which in Taylor's time also

Notes to Pages 47-58   153

means "friend" and "support." All of these definitions are pertinent to the themes and imagery of "Meditation 1.19."

27. Francis Quarles, *Hieroglyphics of the Life of Man* (London, 1638), p. 60.

28. William J. Scheick, "Anonymity and Signature," *Two Mather Biographies; "Life and Death" and "Parentator"* (Bethlehem: Lehigh Univ. Press, 1989), pp. 29-30.

29. Meserole, *American Poetry of the Seventeenth-Century*, pp. 208-20 (stanzas 14, 17, 35).

30. Anthony Somerby, highly educated author of a manuscript version of the Bible in verse, died in November 1686; but he is an improbable candidate for the subject of Taylor's elegy.

31. *The Heroicall Devices of M. Claudius Paradin* (London, 1591), p. 276.

32. Northop Frye, *Anatomy of Criticism: Four Essays* (Princeton: Princeton Univ. Press, 1957), pp. 189-94.

33. On Taylor's sense of the connection between scatological matters and salvation, see Keller, pp. 191-206.

34. See, for example, Increase Mather, *Christ the Fountaine of Life* (London, 1651), p. 145; and Cotton Mather, *Manuductio ad Ministerium* (Boston, 1726), pp. 38-42.

35. Donald E. Stanford, "The Giant Bones of Claverack, New York, 1705," *New York History* 40 (1959): 47-61; *The Minor Poetry of Edward Taylor*, ed. Thomas M. and Virginia L. Davis (Boston: G.K. Hall, 1981), pp. 211-16.

36. Robert Graves, *The Greek Myths* (New York: Braziller, 1959), 1:131-33.

37. Robert Graves and Raphael Patai, *Hebrew Myths: The Book of Genesis* (New York: Greenwich House, 1983), pp. 100-3.

38. In ancient and medieval tradition the serpent, an emblem of Pallas, is depicted as a winged dragon: Margery Corbett and Ronald Lightbrown, *The Comely Frontispiece: The Emblematic Title-Page in England, 1550-1660* (London: Routledge & Kegan Paul, 1979), pp. 71-72.

39. William J. Scheick, "Order and Disorder in Taylor's Poetry: Meditation 1.8," *American Poetry* 5, ii (1988): 2-11.

40. "For out of the serpents roote shal come forthe a cockatrise, and the fruite thereof shalbe a fyrie flying serpent" (Isaiah 14:29). A cockatrice is a legendary deadly serpent hatched by a reptile from a cock's egg on a dunghill. The image of the cock in Taylor's poem, moreover, suggests the conical shape of a heap of dung (termed a cock) as well as the arrogant, crowing nature of the damned and the aggressive, rebellious crowing nature of the scavenger devils. A dunghill cock is *gallus* in Latin, suggesting another pun on the meanings of gall in the poem, as discussed above.

41. Joel R. Kehler, "Physiology and Metaphor in Edward Taylor's 'Meditation. Can. 1.3,'" *Early American Literature* 9 (1975): 315-20.

42. "To the serpent dust shalbe his meat" (Isaiah 65:25). "Feare ye

not them that kil the bodie, but are not able to kil the soule: but rather feare him, which is able to destroye both soule and bodies in hel" (Matt. 10-28).

43. Mildred Fielder, *Plant Medicine and Folklore* (New York: Winchester, 1975), p. 151.

44. On the meaning of this image on Chartres, see Philippe Ariès, *The Hour of Our Death*, trans. Helen Weaver (New York: Vintage, 1982), pp. 101-2.

45. Graves and Patai, pp. 79-81; Sir James G. Frazer, *Folklore in the Old Testament: Studies in Comparative Religion, Legend, and Law* (New York: Macmillan, 1923), pp. 18-20.

46. Catherine Rainwater, "'This Brazen Serpent Is a Doctors Shop': Edward Taylor's Medical Vision," *Studies in Puritan American Spirituality* 2 (1991): 51-76.

47. On Taylor's management of the old and the new astronomy, as well as for an excellent close reading of one of his meditations, see Catherine Rainwater, "Edward Taylor's Reluctant Revolution: The New Astronomy in *Preparatory Meditations*," *American Poetry* 1, ii (1984): 4-17.

48. Ariès, p. 102.

49. This technique is discussed in William J. Scheick, "Typology and Allegory: A Comparative Study of George Herbert and Edward Taylor," *Essays in Literature* 2 (1975): 76-86. See also Rowe, p. 248.

50. Gatta, p. 169.

3. Laughter and Death

1. Some of the traditions informing Puritan humor are suggested by Gatta, *Gracious Laughter*.

2. For example, Carl Holliday, "The First American Satirist," *Sewanee Review* 16 (1908): 315; Roy F. Dibble, "The Simple Cobler of Agawam," *South Atlantic Quarterly* 19 (1920): 163; Lawrence C. Wroth, ed. *The Simple Cobler of Aggawam in America* (New York: SF&R, 1937), p. ii.

3. Although Jean Béranger's *Nathaniel Ward (ca. 1578-1652)* (Bordeaux, France: Sobodi, 1969) treats the work in general terms, Robert D. Arner's "*The Simple Cobler of Aggawam*: Nathaniel Ward's Rhetoric of Satire," *Early American Literature* 5, iii (1970): 3-16, offers some good observations on certain features of Ward's satiric manner.

4. Albert H. Marckwardt, *American English* (New York, Oxford Univ. Press, 1958), p. 101.

5. Relatedly, in "Early Histories of American Literature: A Chapter in the Institution of New England" (*American Literary History* 1 [1989]: 459-88) Nina Baym points out the paradox of American literary histories which have valorized the didactic and moral features of New England colonial writings as a model for American literature,

but which have also denigrated that model as belletristically primitive specifically because of these very same features.

6. *The Simple Cobler of Aggawam in America*, ed. P.M. Zall (Lincoln: Univ. of Nebraska Press, 1969), p. 77. An earlier version of my remarks here appeared as "Nathaniel Ward's Cobbler as 'Shoem-Aker,'" *English Language Notes* 9 (1971): 100-2.

7. On the Puritan regard for Hebrew, see Samuel Eliot Morison, *Harvard College in the Seventeenth Century* (Cambridge: Harvard Univ. Press, 1936), 1:200-7.

8. John W. Dean, *A Memoir of the Rev. Nathaniel Ward* (Albany: J. Munsell, 1868), pp. 10, 27-28; and Béranger, pp. 53-54.

9. Haim Shachter, *The New Universal Hebrew-English Dictionary* (Tel-Aviv, Israel: Yavneh, 1962), 2:747.

10. See William J. Scheick, "The Widower Narrator in Nathaniel Ward's *The Simple Cobler of Aggawam in America*," *New England Quarterly* 47 (1974): 87-96, on which some of the following discussion is based.

11. See, for example, Karen E. Rowe, "Sacred or Profane?: Edward Taylor's Meditations on Canticles," *Modern Philology* 72 (1974): 123-38; and Jeffrey Hammond, "A Puritan *Ars Moriendi*: Edward Taylor's Late Meditations on the Song of Songs," *Early American Literature* 17 (1982): 191-214.

12. Edmund S. Morgan, *The Puritan Family: Religion and Domestic Relations in Seventeenth-Century New England* (New York: Harper & Row, 1966), pp. 41-42.

13. Critics have read this comment as a literal reference to the fact that at the time Ward wrote *The Simple Cobler* he had lived for twelve years in New England. But if Ward arrived in New England in 1634, uncertain is the date of the death of his wife, Elizabeth. John W. Dean's claim that 1634 is the date of her death is based solely on this passage from *The Simple Cobler*, which may or may not make autobiographical revelations, but which is so evidently wrought as an artistic construction that the critic is cautioned against a merely literal reading of any detail in it.

14. However, the excesses of the Parliament's military would cause Ward to come to the king's defense in *A Religious Retreat Sounded to a Religious Army* (1647). Clearly Ward believed in monarchy as a divinely sanctioned hierarchical pattern of social order. All he seeks is a corrective to King Charles's adulteration of divine truth.

15. Morgan, *Puritan Family*, pp. 44-45.

16. *Surcingle* means, among other definitions, a belt worn around the cassock of a clergyman.

17. *Flurt* derives from *fleurettée*, meaning a small flower ornament. Ward's word also puns on *flirt*, which in Ward's time refers to a woman of loose character.

18. *Hood-holes* refers to monks' attire.

19. Morgan, *The Puritan Family*, p. 36.

20. This was not the case in England; see Samuel Eliot Morison, *Builders of the Bay Colony* (Boston: Houghton Mifflin, 1930), p. 220.

21. David Hackett Fischer, *Albion's Seed: Four British Folkways in America* (New York: Oxford Univ. Press, 1989), p. 88.

22. Meserole, *American Poetry of the Seventeenth Century*, pp. 210, 212. My comments here include several observations from my "Standing in the Gap: Urian Oakes's Elegy on Thomas Shephard," *Early American Literature* 9 (1975): 301-6.

23. See Scheick, *The Will and the Word*, pp. 49-90.

24. An awareness of a Puritan stress on the communal more than on the personal is evident, to cite two representative instances, in Edmund S. Morgan's *The Puritan Family*, p. 168; and Cecelia Tichi's "Spiritual Biography and the 'Lords Remembrancers,'" *William and Mary Quarterly* 28 (1971), 69. Specific application of this stress to elegies occurs in Kenneth Silverman's *Colonial American Poetry* (New York: Hafner, 1968), p. 127; and Sacvan Bercovitch's *The Puritan Origins of the American Self* (New Haven: Yale Univ. Press, 1975), pp. 121-22. On the difficulties of drawing generalizations about Puritan elegies and on the effect of the Restoration on the elegiac motif of the collective self, see William J. Scheick, "Tombless Virtue and Hidden Text: New England Puritan Funeral Elegies," *Puritan Poets and Poetics: Seventeenth-Century American Poetry in Theory and Practice*, ed. Peter White (University Park: Pennsylvania State Univ. Press, 1985), pp. 286-302.

25. The extensive stellar imagery in Oakes's poem derives from biblical sanction, as we saw in chapter 2. That in this instance it might also echo of Ben Johnson is suggested by J.A. Leo Lemay, "Johnson and Milton: Two Influences in Oakes's *Elegie*," *New England Quarterly* 38 (1965): 90-92.

26. Throughout his elegy Oakes uses the word *wit* in a double sense, referring to both rational humor and reason itself. On the Puritan use of the Scholastic equation of wit and reason, see John Morgan, *Godly Learning: Puritan Attitudes towards Reason, Learning, and Education, 1560-1640* (Cambridge: Cambridge Univ. Press, 1986), p. 46.

27. Oakes's circumspection concerning the writing of his elegy not only pertains to the pattern of integration I am discussing here but also to the self-consciousness of early Puritans about dishonestly flattering the dead and in the process misguiding the living and to the elegiac convention of bemoaning an inadequacy to perform the task. On the latter matter see, Ruth Wallerstein, *Studies in Seventeenth-Century Poetic* (Madison: Univ. of Wisconsin Press, 1950), p. 83; and T.G. Hahn, "Urian Oakes's *Elegie* on Thomas Shephard and Puritan Poetics," *American Literature* 45 (1973): 168-69. On the former matter, see Increase Mather in Scheick, *Two Mather Biographies*, p. 44; and James Fitch's prefatory remarks to *Peace the End of the Perfect and Uprigh[t]* (Boston, 1672). Concerning Oakes's elegy, Edwin T. Bowden

notes "not just the Augustinian refusal of artificial heightening but the deliberate choice—in origin a rich mixture of the esthetic, the utilitarian and the theological—of the direct and the immediate in style, the parallel in verse of the 'plain style' in prose: "Urian Oakes' *Elegy:* Colonial Literature and History," *Forum* 10, ii (1972): 7.

4. Breaking Verbal Icons

1. See, for example, Edwin H. Cady, "The Artistry of Jonathan Edwards," *New England Quarterly* 22 (1949): 61-72; Willis J. Buckingham, "Stylistic Artistry in the Sermons of Jonathan Edwards," *Papers on Language and Literature* 6 (1970): 136-51; and Annette Kolodny, "Imagery in the Sermons of Jonathan Edwards," *Early American Literature* 7 (1972):172-82.

2. The reading of Edwards as forward-looking has been most comprehensively advanced by Perry Miller, *Jonathan Edwards* (New York: Sloane, 1949); Alan Heimert, *Religion and the American Mind from the Great Awakening to the Revolution* (Cambridge: Harvard Univ. Press, 1966); and Sang Hyun Lee, *The Philosophical Theology of Jonathan Edwards* (Princeton: Princeton Univ. Press, 1988).

3. Peter Gay, *A Loss of Mastery: Puritan Historians in Colonial America* (New York: Vintage, 1968), p. 116.

4. *Religious Affections*, ed. John E. Smith (New Haven: Yale Univ. Press, 1959), pp. 1-83.

5. However, the first generation of New England ministers found the institution of the spiritual relation a controversial issue: see, for example, Baird Tipson, "Samuel Stone's 'Discourse' against Requiring Church Relations," *William and Mary Quarterly* 46 (1989): 786-99. On the early and late controversies surrounding the baptism of children, see Robert G. Pope, *The Half-Way Covenant: Church Membership in Puritan New England* (Princeton: Princeton Univ. Press, 1969).

6. The cornerstone of the arguments for Locke's major influence on Edwards is Perry Miller's *Jonathan Edwards*. For the range of the discussion of this ongoing debate, see M.X. Lesser, *Jonathan Edwards: A Reference Guide* (Boston: G.K. Hall, 1981).

7. A revisionist anti-Lockean reading of Edwards is provided by Norman Fiering, *Jonathan Edwards's Moral Thought and its British Context* (Chapel Hill: Univ. of North Carolina Press, 1981).

8. For a thorough discussion of Edward's idealism, see Michael J. Colacurcio, "The Example of Edwards: Idealist Imagination and the Metaphysics of Sovereignty," *Puritan Influences in American Literature*, ed. Emory Elliott (Urbana: Univ. of Illinois Press, 1979), pp. 55-106. See also Fiering, *Jonathan Edwards's Moral Thought*, p. 39.

9. *The Works of President Edwards*, ed. Sereno E. Dwight (New York: Carvill, 1830), 5:349.

10. *The Great Awakening*, ed. C.C. Goen (New Haven: Yale Univ.

158 *Notes to Pages 92-96*

Press, 1972), p. 386. The date of the publication of *Some Thoughts* is 1743, not the usually assigned date of 1742.

11. See, for example, *The Art of Prophesying: New England Sermons and the Shaping of Belief* (Athens: Univ. of Georgia Press, 1987), in which Teresa Toulouse indicates how a contemporary of Edwards, Benjamin Colman, expanded the traditional model of the Puritan sermon nearly to the breaking point by accommodating eighteenth-century secular claims (such as self-interest) within a seventeenth-century theological framework.

12. *The Writings of Thomas Paine*, ed. M.D. Conway (New York: Putnam, 1896), 4:55.

13. See John Morgan, *Godly Learning: Puritan Attitudes towards Reason, Learning, and Education, 1560-1640* (Cambridge: Cambridge Univ. Press, 1986), pp. 48, 57.

14. See, for example, Edward H. Davidson, *Jonathan Edwards: A Narrative of the Puritan Mind* (Cambridge: Harvard Univ. Press, 1968); and Clyde A. Holbrook, *Jonathan Edwards, The Valley and Nature: An Interpretative Essay* (Lewisburg: Bucknell Univ. Press, 1987). In *Nature and Religious Imagination: From Edwards to Bushnell* (Philadelphia: Fortress Press, 1980) Conrad Cherry offers the helpful observation that Edwards approached nature less as literal signs sensately indicative of a didactic moralism (as they became for Edwards's New Divinity disciples) than as symbols re-presenting a spiritual sense of the ultimate reality they signify.

15. David Scofield Wilson, "The Flying Spider," *Journal of the History of Ideas* 32 (1971): 447-58.

16. *Images or Shadows of Divine Things*, ed. Perry Miller (New Haven: Yale Univ. Press, 1948), p. 61.

17. Samuel Hopkins, *The Life and Character of the Late Reverend Mr. Jonathan Edwards*, in *Jonathan Edwards: A Profile* (New York: Hill and Wang, 1969), pp. 24-39.

18. Quotations from this sermon are derived from *The Works of President Edwards*, ed. Samuel Austin (Worchester, Mass.: Isaiah Thomas, 1808-1889), 8:290-312.

19. Determining the exact dates of the first presentation of Edwards's sermons of the 1730s is a complex undertaking complicated by a number of factors, including Edwards's delivery of some of these works on more than one occasion, his cannibalization of his own work, and his handwriting. We must await the Yale edition of these sermons for a clarification of the record in this regard as well as for definitive editions of these writings. See Thomas A. Schafer, "Manuscript Problems in the Yale Edition of Jonathan Edwards," *Early American Literature* 3 (1968): 159-71.

20. Quotations from this sermon are derived from *Works* (Austin) 7:208-27.

21. *Works* (Dwight) 7:14. Perhaps it is pertinent to note, as well, that in the 1730s Edwards specifically modified the sermonic pattern

by eliminating a distinct section of "reasons": see John F. Wilson, ed. *The Writings of Jonathan Edwards: A History of the Work of Redemption* (New Haven: Yale Univ. Press, 1989), pp. 35-36.

22. See John West Davidson, *The Logic of Millennial Thought: Eighteenth-Century New England* (New Haven: Yale Univ. Press, 1977); and Nathan O. Hatch, *The Sacred Cause of Liberty: Republican Thought and the Millennium in Revolutionary New England* (New Haven: Yale Univ. Press, 1977).

23. *The Workes of Reverend Richard Greenham*, ed. Henry Holland (London, 1612), p. 646. See also Richard Rogers, *Seven Treatises, Containing Such Direction As Is Gathered out of the Holie Scriptures* (London, 1603), p. 4; and Thomas Adams, *The Workes of Thomas Adams* (London, 1630), p. 406.

24. On the aesthetic philosophy behind this idea, see Roland André Delattre, *Beauty and Sensibility in the Thought of Jonathan Edwards: An Essay in Aesthetics and Theological Ethics* (New Haven: Yale Univ. Press, 1968). In *Jonathan Edwards: Art and the Sense of the Heart* (Amherst: Univ. of Massachusetts Press, 1980) Terrence Erdt argues, contrary to the direction of my discussion here, that because of his aesthetic philosophy Edwards had a positive attitude toward verbal artistry.

25. Although Edwards's skepticism about language seems to have endured throughout his career, his attitude toward nature possibly mutated over time. See, for example, Clyde A. Holbrook, *Jonathan Edwards, The Valley and Nature;* and William J. Scheick, *The Writings of Jonathan Edwards: Theme, Motif, and Style* (College Station: Texas A&M Univ. Press, 1975).

26. See E. Brooks Holifield, *The Covenant Sealed: The Development of Puritan Sacramental Theology in Old and New England, 1570-1720* (New Haven: Yale Univ. Press, 1974).

27. *Some Thoughts*, p. 386.

28. *Ethical Writings*, ed. Paul Ramsey (New Haven: Yale Univ. Press, 1989), pp. 462-63.

29. See Perry Miller, "The Rhetoric of Sensation," *Errand into the Wilderness* (New York: Harper & Row, 1964), pp. 167-83; and Edward H. Davidson, "From Locke to Edwards," *Journal of the History of Ideas* 24 (1963): 355-72. On Edwards's sense of the separation between signifier and signified, see Douglas J. Elwood, *The Philosophical Theology of Jonathan Edwards* (New York: Columbus Univ. Press, 1960), pp. 166-67.

30. *Freedom of the Will*, ed. Paul Ramsey (New Haven: Yale Univ. Press, 1957), p. 376.

31. Quotations from this sermon are derived from *Works* (Austin) 7:467-85.

32. On Edward's modifications in sermonic form, see Wilson H. Kimnach, "The Brazen Trumpet: Jonathan Edwards's Conception of the Sermon," *Jonathan Edwards: His Life and Influence*, ed. Charles

Angoff (Rutherford, N.J.: Fairleigh Dickinson Univ. Press, 1975), pp. 29-44.

33. Quotations from this sermon are derived from *Works* (Dwight) 5:473-76.

34. During the Great Awakening, the religious revival of the 1740s, however, Edwards will reemploy the image of the family in a much more positive manner: see William J. Scheick, "Family, Conversion, and the Self in Jonathan Edwards' *A Faithful Narrative of the Surprising Work of God,*" *Tennessee Studies in Literature* 19 (1974): 79-89.

35. Quotations from this sermon are derived from *Works* (Austin) 7:267-307.

36. Quotations from this sermon are derived from *Works* (Austin) 7:326-74.

37. For an excellent discussion of how several English poets forged a space for creativity within the iconoclastic tradition, see Ernest B. Gilman, *Iconoclasm and Poetry in the English Reformation: Down Went Dagon* (Chicago: Univ. of Chicago Press, 1986).

5. Islands of Meaning

1. Arthur O. Lewis, Jr., ed. *American Utopias: Selected Short Fiction* (New York: Arno Press & The New York Times, 1971), p. vii. An earlier version of my remarks here appeared as "'An Allegorical Description of a Certain Island and its Inhabitants': Eighteenth-Century Parable or Satire?" *New England Quarterly* 63 (1990): 468-74. Nathan Fiske makes several appearances in John Brooke's *The Heart of the Commonweath: Society and Political Culture in Worcester County, Massachusetts, 1713-1861* (Cambridge: Cambridge Univ. Press, 1989), on which I have relied for information on Fiske.

2. Most recently, Donald Weber, *Rhetoric and History in Revolutionary New England* (New York: Oxford Univ. Press, 1988).

3. Lewis, p. vii.

4. Lewis, p. vii.

5. Thomas Paine, *Common Sense* (Garden City, N.Y.: Doubleday, 1960), p. 42.

6. Bruce Granger, *American Essay Serials from Franklin to Irving* (Knoxville: Univ. of Tennessee Press, 1978), p. 164.

7. Edward E. Chielens (ed.), *American Literary Magazines: The Eighteenth and Nineteenth-Centuries* (New York: Greenwood Press, 1986), pp. 244-45.

8. Benjamin Franklin V, ed., *Boston Printers, Publishers, and Booksellers: 1640-1800* (Boston: G.K. Hall, 1980), p. 464.

9. Franklin, p. 470.

10. See Alan Heimert, *Religion and the American Mind from the Great Awakening to the Revolution* (Cambridge: Harvard Univ. Press, 1966).

11. Bernard Bailyn, *The Ideological Origins of the American Revolution* (Cambridge: Harvard Univ. Press, 1973), pp. 119-30.

12. Doreen Alvarez Saar, "Crèvecoeur's 'Thoughts on Slavery': *Letters from an American Farmer* and Whig Rhetoric," *Early American Literature* 22 (1987): 192-203.

13. Bailyn, *Ideological*, p. 233.

14. Scheick, *Two Mather Biographies: "Life and Death" and "Parentator"*, p. 138.

15. William J. Scheick, "Tombless Virtue and Hidden Text: New England Puritan Funeral Elegies," *Puritan Poets and Poetics: Seventeenth-Century American Poetry in Theory and Practice*, ed. Peter White (University Park: Pennsylvania State Univ. Press, 1985), p. 290.

16. Bernard Bailyn, *Voyagers to the West: A Passage in the Peopling of America on the Eve of the Revolution* (New York: Knopf, 1986), pp. 172-75, 193-95.

17. Bailyn, *Voyagers*, pp. 173-74.

18. J.A. Leo Lemay, ed., *Benjamin Franklin: Writings* (New York: Library of America, 1987), pp. 357-58, 525-26.

19. A. Roger Ekirch, *Bound for America: The Transportation of British Convicts to the Colonies 1718-1775* (Oxford: Oxford Univ. Press, 1987), pp. 68, 131.

20. Ekirch, pp. 63, 151.

21. Ekirch, p. 221.

22. Robert Hughes, *The Fatal Shore* (New York: Knopf, 1986), pp. 98-99.

23. Lemay, p. 1144.

24. Lewis, pp. xv-xvi. An earlier version of my comments here appeared as "The Letter Killeth: Edward Bellamy's 'To Whom This May Come,'" *American Utopias: Texts and Contexts*, ed. Jean Pfaelzer, *American Transcendental Quarterly* 3 (1989): 55-67.

25. Arthur E. Morgan, *Edward Bellamy* (New York: Columbia Univ. Press, 1944), pp. 191-98.

26. Robert E. Hogan, "*Dr. Heidenhoff's Process* and *Miss Ludington's Sister*: Edward Bellamy's Romances of Immortality," *Studies in American Fiction* 8 (1980): 51-68; Hans-Joachim Lang, "Looking Backward at the Second Revolution in Massachusetts: Edward Bellamy's *The Duke of Stockbridge* as Historical Romance," *Amerikastudien* 28 (1983): 309-322; Olaf Hansen, "Edward Bellamy: *Looking Backward: 2000-1887* (1888)," *Die Utopie in der Angloamerikanischen Literatur*, ed. Hartmut Heurmann and Berna-Peter Lange (Düsseldorf: Schwann-Bagel, 1984), pp. 103-19. The influence of predecessors is not always beneficial, and possibly in the instance of *Looking Backward* and other utopian fiction, the romance form inherited by writers such as Bellamy often imposes limitations on the transformative design of these works: Jean Pfaelzer, *The Utopian Novel in America, 1886-1896: The Politics of Form* (Pittsburgh: Univ. of Pittsburgh Press, 1984), p. 41.

27. Joseph L. Blau, "Bellamy's Religious Motivation for Social Reform: A Review-Article," *Review of Religion* 21 (1957): 156-66; Joseph Schiffman, "Edward Bellamy's Religious Thought," *PMLA* 68 (1953): 716-32. For a particularly insightful reading of Bellamy's appropriation of the biblical model of conversion to promote a radical utopian transformation of the self, see Jeffrey A. Hammond, "'Swept Away by one Breath': Selfhood and *Kenosis* in Edward Bellamy's 'A Love Story Reversed,'" *Texas Studies in Literature and Language* 32 (1990): 329-44.

28. Edward Bellamy, *The Blindman's World and Other Stories* (Boston: Houghton, Mifflin, 1898), pp. 404, 405, 411. This text of "To Whom This May Come" does not differ from the first edition in *Harper's New Monthly Magazine* 78 (Feb. 1889).

29. Graves and Patai, *Hebrew Myths: The Book of Genesis*, p. 129.

30. Joseph Schiffman, ed., "Introduction," *Edward Bellamy: Selected Writings on Religion and Society* (New York: Liberal Arts Press, 1955), pp. xvi-xvii; John L. Thomas, ed., *Looking Backward 2000-1887* (Cambridge: Harvard Univ. Press, 1967), p. 13.

31. On the problematic nature of the ontology of this self, especially in relation to time, see Janet Gabler-Hover's valuable "Man's Fragile Tenure: Discontinuous Time and the Ethos of Temporality in Edward Bellamy's Short Fiction," *Texas Studies in Literature and Language* 32 (1990): 302-28.

32. Lawrence I. Buell, *Literary Transcendentalism: Style and Vision in the American Renaissance* (Ithaca: Cornell Univ. Press, 1973); William J. Scheick, *The Slender Human Word: Emerson's Artistry in Prose* (Knoxville: Univ. of Tennessee Press, 1978).

33. Robert E. Spiller and Alfred R. Ferguson, eds., *The Collected Works of Ralph Waldo Emerson: Volume I, Nature, Addresses, and Lectures* (Cambridge: Harvard Univ. Press, 1971), p. 17.

34. Spiller and Ferguson, p. 65.

35. William J. Scheick, *Fictional Structure and Ethics: The Turn-of-the-Century English Novel* (Athens: Univ. of Georgia Press, 1990).

36. See Philip F. Gura, *The Wisdom of Words: Language, Theology, and Literature in the New England Renaissance* (Middletown: Wesleyan Univ. Press, 1981).

37. Herman Melville, *Mardi*, ed. Harrison Hayford, Hershel Parker, and G. Thomas Tanselle (Evanston: Northwestern Univ. Press, 1970), pp. 269, 507. See also James Duban, *Melville's Major Fiction: Politics, Theology, and Imagination* (Dekalb: Northern Illinois Univ. Press, 1983), p. 254.

38. See, for example, John T. Irwin, *American Hieroglyphics: The Symbol of the Egyptian Hieroglyphics in the American Renaissance* (New Haven: Yale Univ. Press, 1980); William J. Scheick, "The Hieroglyphic Rock in Hawthorne's 'Roger Malvin's Burial,'" *ESQ: A Journal of the American Renaissance* 24 (1978): 72-76.

39. *Looking Backward*, pp. 119, 189-91, 198.

40. *Looking Backward,* p. 298.
41. *Looking Backward,* p. 271.
42. Edward Bellamy, "How I Came to Write 'Looking Backward,' " *The Nationalist* 1, i (May 1889): 1-4.
43. Edward Bellamy, "How I Wrote 'Looking Backward,' " *Ladies Home Journal* 11, v (Apr. 1894): 2.
44. Sylvia E. Bowman, *The Year 2000: A Critical Biography of Edward Bellamy* (New York: Bookman, 1958); Bowman, *Edward Bellamy Abroad: An American Prophet's Influence* (New York: Twayne, 1962).
45. Morgan, p. 230.
46. Morgan, pp. 245-46.
47. Morgan, p. 187.
48. Schiffman, "Edward Bellamy's Religious Thought," 716-32.
49. In his introductory comments to *The Blindman's World and Other Stories* William Dean Howells explains that Bellamy's "distinctive virtue" was the possession of an "imagination which revived throughout Christiandom the faith in a millennium" (p. vi).
50. Morgan, p. 248.
51. Some readers might sense a subversive pessimistic undercurrent in Bellamy's management of the narrator's death, and indeed some critics have detected (as I have as well in the above discussion) certain unintentional traces of pessimism even in Bellamy's novel: for example, Tom H. Towers, "The Insomnia of Julian West," *American Literature* 47 (1975): 52-63. Such may be the case, but it is also important to remember that the theme of death as transformative in redeeming the unregenerate is a frequent theme of nineteenth-century popular fiction and religious literature (Jane Tompkins, *Sensational Designs: The Cultural Work of American Fiction, 1790-1860* [New York: Oxford Univ. Press, 1985], pp. 122-46) and that death is a ready Christian metaphor in *Looking Backward* for a humanity that does not live in the spirit of its potentiality. So West speaks of "wretched beings" who are "all quite dead," "their bodies . . . so many living sepulchers" with "a soul dead within" (*Looking Backward,* pp. 305-6). Bellamy's short story, "The Cold Snap" (1875), is also an allegory about how the heart can be threatened by a death of the spirit.

Index

Abel (biblical character), 38
Abraham (biblical character), 108
Adam (biblical character), 21, 36-40, 45-62, 77, 81, 96-97, 102, 132-33
Alciati, Andreae, 59-60; *Emblemata*, 59
Alexander the Great, 59
Allerton, Isaac, 9
American Utopias, 130
Ames, William, 91
Anglicanism, 21, 76, 97-98
Antaeus (mythic figure), 51
Augustine, 2-3, 20-23, 68, 98, 101, 118

Bay Psalm Book, The, 24
Bellamy, Edward, 4, 130-45; *Blindman's World, The*, 130; *Looking Backward*, 130, 136-40, 144; "Religion of Solidarity," 139; "To Whom This May Come," 130-45; *Talks on Nationalism*, 131
Body of Liberties, 79
Bradford, William, 4, 6-19, 24-27, 33-34, 61, 63, 65, 69, 72-74, 87, 89, 129; *Of Plymouth Plantation*, 6-18
Bradstreet, Anne, 4, 29, 32-45, 55, 67, 69, 72, 79, 86, 89, 93-94, 98, 116, 118, 145; "Contemplations," 32-44, 67, 86; "On My Dear Grand Child," 44
Bradstreet, Simon, 44
Brewster, William, 14
Bunyan, John, 103, 112; *Pilgrim's Progress*, 103, 112
Bushnell, Horace, 135

Cain (biblical character), 38
Calvinism, 98-99, 129, 140, 144
Charles I, King, 72-81
Charles II, King, 126
Chartres (cathedral), 59-60
Cleland, John, 124; *Memoirs of a Woman of Pleasure*, 124
Covenant of Grace, 25-26, 55, 62
Covenant of Works, 25-26, 55, 62
Crèvecoeur, Hector St. John de, 126; *Letters from an American Farmer*, 126

Danforth II, Samuel, 22
Darwinism, 134-35
David (biblical character), 24, 54, 83
Deism, 92, 124-25

Edwards, Jonathan, 4, 89-119, 143, 145; *Careful and Strict Enquiry into . . . Freedom of the Will, A*, 101; "Christian Pilgrim, The." *See* "The True

Index 165

Christian's Life"; "Dissertation Concerning the End," 100; *Divine and Supernatural Light, A,* 94-97, 99, 117; "Excellency of Christ, The," 110-13, 116; *God Glorified,* 102; *Humble Inquiry, An,* 99; "Justice of God, The," 113-17; "Man's Natural Blindness," 95; "Of Insects," 93; "Personal Narrative," 94, 100; "Pressing into the Kingdom," 103-8, 110; *Some Thoughts,* 92, 100; *Treatise Concerning Religious Affections, A,* 91; "True Christian's Life, The," 94, 108-10;
emblems, 30-34, 36, 39-45, 55-61, 66, 69, 73, 80, 115, 117
Emerson, Ralph Waldo, 134-36; *American Scholar, The,* 134
Eve (biblical character), 36, 77, 81, 132-33
Ezekiel (biblical prophet), 116

Fabius Maximus, Quintus, 16
Fiske, John, 135
Fiske, Nathan, 4, 121-29, 144-45; "Allegorical Description, An," 121-29; *Moral Monitor, The,* 124; *Sermon Preached at the Dudleian Lecture,* 125
Franklin, Benjamin, 127-28
Freneau, Philip, 126-27; "America Independent," 126; *British Prison Ship, The,* 127

Galenic medicine, 58
Ge (mythic figure), 51
George III, King, 122, 123
George, Saint, 48
Greenham, Richard, 96

Hannibal, 16
Hawthorne, Nathaniel, 130-31, 135, 143; *Scarlet Letter, The,* 135

Henrietta, Maria, Queen, 76-78
Hercules (mythic figure), 51-55, 57, 59, 66
Hesperides (mythic place), 53
Horace, 24, 72; *Odes,* 72

Israel, 9

Jefferson, Thomas, 125-26; *Declaration of Independence,* 125; "Summary View, The," 125-26
John the Baptist, 104, 106, 107
Johnson, Bryon, 135
Johnson, Thomas H., 30
Jonah (biblical prophet), 18
Jove (mythic figure), 17, 60. *See also* Zeus

LaCapra, Dominick, 1
Ladon (mythic figure), 53
Laud, Archbishop William, 17
Laudians, 21
Leonidas, 83-84
Lewis, Arthur O., 130
Locke, John, 91-93, 96, 101-2
logogic crux, logogic site (defined), 2-3, 120-21
London Chronicle, The, 127
Loyalists, 129
Lutheranism, 99
Lyford, John, 12

Manicheanism, 27
Massachusetts Magazine, 121, 123-26
Mather, Cotton, 126
Mather, Increase, 23
Mather, Richard, 4, 6, 23-29, 33-34, 45, 79, 85, 89, 118
Mather, Samuel, 3
Melville, Herman, 135; *Mardi,* 135
memory, 2, 37-44, 82, 86, 92, 108, 128
Miller, J. Hillis, 1
Miller, Perry, 19, 24

Morton, Thomas, 4, 6, 15-18, 34, 43, 69, 79, 144; *New English Canaan*, 15-18, 79
Moses (biblical character), 87

Narragansetts, 9
Nationalist Club, 137, 140
necessity (providential), 6-18
New Nation, The, 131
New York Tribune, 138
Nietzsche, Friedrich, 135
Nora, Pierre, 2

Oakes, Uriah, 4, 47, 68-69, 80-89, 108, 110, 118; *Elegie upon . . . Thomas Shepard, An*, 68-69, 80-88
Oldham, John, 12

Paine, Thomas, 92-93, 125-26; *Age of Reason, The*, 92-93; *Crisis, The*, 126
Paul, Saint, 72, 78, 114, 139-41, 144
Peirce, John, 7
Pennsylvania Gazette, The, 127
Philanthropist (pseudonym), 121
Pilgrims, 6-18
Plato, 10-11, 133
Poseidon, 51
Psalms, 24, 83

Quarles, Francis, 47, 59-60, 63; *Emblems*, 59, 63

Ramism, 24-25
Reformed tradition, 19-24, 29, 68, 145
Renaissance tradition, 18-24, 29, 48, 52, 59, 62, 68, 93, 98, 101, 145
Reynolds, Captain, 9
rhetoric, 19-20, 24-29, 72, 78, 83, 97, 108-10, 123, 128
Ricoeur, Paul, 32
Robinson, John, 14

Roman Catholicism, 21, 30, 76, 78, 99

sapientia, 21, 24, 36-37, 49, 95-103, 107, 111, 113, 117-19, 143
Sarah (biblical character), 108
Satan, 4, 6, 19, 24-29, 34, 48, 51, 53, 61-66, 72, 83, 133
Saturday Review (London), 138
Schopenhauer, Arthur, 135
scientia, 21, 24, 36-37, 49, 95-103, 106, 109-13, 117-19, 143
Shea, Daniel B., 17
Shepard, Thomas (1605-1649), 91
Shepard, Thomas (1635-1677), 47, 80-87
Spenser, Herbert, 135
Springfield Union, 131

Taylor, Edward, 4, 6, 23-29, 30-34, 45-67, 69, 72-73, 81, 83, 89, 98, 106, 116, 118, 145; *Christographia*, 27; *Gods Determinations*, 24-29, 55, 61, 83; "Meditation 1.7," 23; "Meditation 1.8," 37, 49, 56; "Meditation 1.19," 33-34, 45-67, 81; "Meditation 2.61," 60; "Meditation 2.106," 23; *Preparatory Meditations*, 30-31, 33, 98
Thomas, Isaiah, 125-29
Tower of Babel (as image), 3, 34-35, 37-38, 41, 43, 46, 55, 65, 67, 73, 79-80, 86, 111-12, 119, 132, 134, 142, 145
Transcendentalism, 134-36, 139
Transportation Act, 127
Trojan horse (as image), 16, 27-28, 34, 79, 118, 144
typology, 3, 31, 51-54, 65

Ward, Nathaniel, 4, 68-81, 84-85, 87-89, 108, 110, 118,

145; *Religious Retreat, A,* 155 n. 14; *Simple Cobler, The,* 69-80, 84, 88
Washington, George, 126; "Address to the Continental Army," 126
Weber, Max, 145
Whitman, Walt, 134; "Noiseless Patient Spider," 134

Wigglesowth, Michael, 40; "Short Discourse on Eternity, A," 40
Willard, Cyrus Field, 140

Young, Edward, 122-23; *Night Thoughts,* 122

Zeus, 51. *See also* Jove

www.ingramcontent.com/pod-product-compliance
Lightning Source LLC
Chambersburg PA
CBHW032048150426
43194CB00006B/453